Florever Wherever

Florever Wherever

Floral inspiration from all over the world

stichting
kunstboek

Love

Love makes the world go round. If there is one universal emotion uniting people all around the world it has to be love. And the fact that one needs a good party now and then. Wedding design and event planning have become big business. Lovebirds all around the world are looking for their unique wedding party and no costs or expenses are saved for that one special day. With their power to convey profound human emotions and thoughts better than any other object, flowers are a big part of the deal. The rose, eternal and universal symbol of romantic love and desire, still topping the list of most beloved flowers.

Florists are on a constant hunt for new inspiration to combine the ancient wedding rituals with cutting-edge floral design. Conceptualizing a dream is the weighty task on a florist's shoulders. Looking across the borders is one way of finding fresh inspiration and extraordinary ideas. Wedding inspiration is going beyond 'something new, something borrowed and something blue...'.
This book is a treasure trove of outstanding wedding ideas and sparkling creativity from all over the world. Thirteen international floral designers are showcasing their most precious wedding designs, from Bohemian chic to classic fairy tale romance, from rock-and-roll bravura to folklore inspired weddings under a starlit Russian sky.

A wondrous emporium of visual delights, both for florists and for everyone hearing the wedding bells ring.

ROBERT KOENE [Greece]

Σ' αγαπώ

p6: Asparagus asparagoides 'Myrtifolius' (Smilax) | Asparagus setaceus | Convallaria majalis | Hydrangea macrophylla 'Schneeball' | Paoenia lactiflora 'Duchesse de Nemours' | Rosa 'White Naomi!' | Zantedeschia 'White Mirage'

p8: Asparagus asparagoides 'Myrtifolius' (Smilax) | Phalaenopsis 'Nagasaki' | Stachys byzantina | Typha (leaves) | Vanda (roots)

p9: Asparagus setaceus | Chrysanthemum 'Feeling White' | Hydrangea macrophylla 'Schneeball' | Phalaenopsis 'Nagasaki' | Viburnum opulus 'Roseum'

Hydrangea 'Green Emerald' | Hydrangea macrophylla 'Schneeball' | Rosa 'White Naomi!' | Viburnum opulus 'Roseum' | steelgrass

Hydrangea 'Green Emerald' | Hydrangea macrophylla 'Schneeball' | Rosa 'White Naomi!' | Viburnum opulus 'Roseum' | steelgrass

p14: Asparagus asparagoides 'Myrtifolius' (Smilax) |
Convallaria majalis | Zantedeschia 'White Mirage' |
steelgrass'
p15: Aspidistra (leaves) | Dendrobium orchids
Location: Porto Elounda Hotel

p16: Dendrobium orchids | Phalaenopsis 'Kobe' | Stachys byzantina
p17: Ficinea fascicularis | Zantedeschia 'Crystal Blush'

p18: Rosa 'White Naomi!'
p19: Convallaria majalis

Я тебя люблю

ELENA ANTIPINA [Russia]

Centaurea cyanus 'Blue Ball' | Centaurea cyanus 'Blue Diadem' | Delphinium consolida 'Giant Imperial' | Euonymus europaeus | Hydrangea arborescens 'Annabelle' | Lathyrus odoratus | Malus coronaria 'Charlottae' | Phlox maculata | Rosa 'Pascali' | Scabiosa 'Blue Moon' | Scabiosa 'Monarch Cockade' | Scabiosa atropurpurea 'Rose Cockade' | Sedum spectabile 'Meteor' | Typha | Viburnum opulus | Viola hybrid 'Blue

Centaurea cyanus 'Blue Ball' | Centaurea cyanus 'Blue Diadem' | Delphinium consolida 'Giant Imperial' | Euonymus europaeus | Hydrangea arborescens 'Annabelle' | Lathyrus odoratus | Malus coronaria 'Charlottae' | Phlox maculata | Rosa 'Pascali' | Scabiosa 'Blue Moon' | Scabiosa 'Monarch Cockade' | Scabiosa atropurpurea 'Rose Cockade' | Sedum spectabile 'Meteor' | Typha | Viburnum opulus | Viola hybrid 'Blue

Centaurea cyanus 'Blue Ball' | Centaurea cyanus 'Blue Diadem' | Delphinium consolida 'Giant Imperial' | Euonymus europaeus | Hydrangea arborescens 'Annabelle' | Lathyrus odoratus | Malus coronaria 'Charlottae' | Phlox maculata | Rosa 'Pascali' | Scabiosa 'Blue Moon' | Scabiosa 'Monarch Cockade' | Scabiosa atropurpurea 'Rose Cockade' | Sedum spectabile 'Meteor' | Typha | Viburnum opulus | Viola hybrid 'Blue

Centaurea cyanus 'Blue Ball' | Centaurea cyanus 'Blue Diadem' | Delphinium consolida 'Giant Imperial' | Euonymus europaeus | Hydrangea arborescens 'Annabelle' | Lathyrus odoratus | Malus coronaria 'Charlottae' | Phlox maculata | Rosa 'Pascali' | Scabiosa 'Blue Moon' | Scabiosa 'Monarch Cockade' | Scabiosa atropurpurea 'Rose Cockade' | Sedum spectabile 'Meteor' | Typha | Viburnum opulus | Viola hybrid 'Blue

Centaurea cyanus 'Blue Ball' | Centaurea cyanus 'Blue Diadem' | Delphinium consolida 'Giant Imperial' | Euonymus europaeus | Hydrangea arborescens 'Annabelle' | Lathyrus odoratus | Malus coronaria 'Charlottae' | Phlox maculata | Rosa 'Pascali' | Scabiosa 'Blue Moon' | Scabiosa 'Monarch Cockade' | Scabiosa atropurpurea 'Rose Cockade' | Sedum spectabile 'Meteor' | Typha | Viburnum opulus | Viola hybrid 'Blue

Centaurea cyanus 'Blue Ball' | Centaurea cyanus 'Blue Diadem' | Delphinium consolida 'Giant Imperial' | Euonymus europaeus | Hydrangea arborescens 'Annabelle' | Lathyrus odoratus | Malus coronaria 'Charlottae' | Phlox maculata | Rosa 'Pascali' | Scabiosa 'Blue Moon' | Scabiosa 'Monarch Cockade' | Scabiosa atropurpurea 'Rose Cockade' | Sedum spectabile 'Meteor' | Typha | Viburnum opulus | Viola hybrid 'Blue'

MARK PAMPLING [Australia]

p36: Banksia menziesii | Berzelia languinosa | Cuscata australis | Dianthus caryophyllus | Dryandra formosa | Eucalyptus (bark) | Leucadendron 'Silvan Red' | Solanum mauritanium

p37: Berzelia languinosa | Calathea lutea | Cornus sericea | Cymbidium 'Lumines' | Dianthus caryophyllus | Eucalyptus (bark) | Leucadendron 'Silvan Red' | Solanum mauritianum | Xanthorrhoea australis,

Cuscuta australis | Cymbidium 'Lumines' | Eucalyptus (bark) | Zantedeschia 'Pink Persuasion'

p 39a: Cymbidium 'Lumines' | Eucalyptus (bark) | Xanthorrhoea australis | Zantedeschia 'Pink Persuasion'
p 39b: Calathea lutea | Cornus sericea | Cymbidium 'Lumines' | Dianthus caryophyllus | Dryandra formosa | Eucalyptus (bark) |
Leucadendron 'Silvan Red' | Solanum mauritianum | Xanthorrhoea australis

THEA KORNHERR [Germany]

Agapanthus praecox | Ceropegia woodii | Gerbera jamesonii | Miscanthus | Odonthoglossum-Hybriden | Ophiopogon | Passiflora caerula | Phalaenopsis | Pilea nummulariifolia | Rhipsalis | Sandersonia aurantiaca | Thunbergia

Agapanthus praecox | Ceropegia woodii | Gerbera jamesonii | Miscanthus | Odonthoglossum-Hybriden | Ophiopogon |
Passiflora caerula | Phalaenopsis | Pilea nummulariifolia | Rhipsalis | Sandersonia aurantiaca | Thunbergia

Bidens ferulifolia | Calendula officinalis | Centaurea cyanus | Convolvulus | Cosmos bipinnatus | Dianthus barbatus | Gerbera jamesonii | Kalanchoe blossfeldiana | Nermesia-Hybriden | Phlox paniculata (hybr) | Rosa | Sanvitalia procumbens | Tagetes patula (hybr) | Tanacetum vulgare | Verbena bonariensis | Zinnia elegans

p48: Ceropegia woodii | Pilea nummulariifolia | orchid
p49: Asparagus asparagoides | Convolvulus | Gerbera jamesonii | Phalaenopsis Phlox paniculata (hybr) | Sandersonia aurantiaca

Anthirrinum majus | Calendula | Centaurea cyanus | Chrysanthemum segetum | Convolvulus | Cosmos bipinnatus | Hydrangea | Panicum | Tagetes patula (hybr) |
Tanacetum vulgare | Zinnia elegans

Asclepias tuberosa | Calendula officinalis | Clematis | Cosmos bipinnatus | Dahlia (hybr) | Delphinium (hybr) | Delphinium (hybr) | Dipladenia | Fagus sylvatica | Foeniculum vulgare | Gloriosa rothschildiana | Miscanthus | Phlox paniculata (hybr) | Sandersonia aurantiaca

Asclepias tuberosa | Calendula officinalis | Clematis | Cosmos bipinnatus | Dahlia (hybr) | Delphinium (hybr) | Delphinium (hybr) | Dipladenia |
Fagus sylvatica | Foeniculum vulgare | Gloriosa rothschildiana | Miscanthus | Phlox paniculata (hybr) | Sandersonia aurantiaca

GARY KWOK [Hong Kong]

p 56-59: Convallaria majalis | Liriope | Ornithogalum | Muscari | Nigella

p60-61: Convallaria majalis | Liriope | Ornithogalum | Muscari | Nigella

Gypsophila, Hydrangea, Paeonia, Rosa sp.

p64-65: Cotinus coggygria, Dianthus, Hydrangea, Rosa sp, Scabiosa

p66-67: Cotinus coggygria, Dianthus, Hydrangea, Rosa sp, Scabiosa

GIORDANO SIMONELLI [Italy]

p 68: Diplocyclos palmatus | Hedera helix | Malus | Panicum | Phalaenopsis 'Texas' | Senecio rowleyanus | Setaria 'Red Jewels' | Zantedeschia 'Red Sox'
p 70: Actinidia sinensis | Allium sativum var. ophioscorodon | Arum italicum | Diplocyclos palmatus | Illicium verum | Juncus spiralis | Malus | Phalaenopsis 'Texas' | Rosa 'Romantica' | Sedum acre | Sertaria 'Red Jewels' | Zantedeschia 'Red Sox'
p 71: Hedera helix | Malus | Senecio rowleyanus | Zantedeschia 'Red Sox'

p72: Anthurium andreanum | Diplocyclos palmatus | Hypericum | Juncus spiralis | Malus | Setaria 'Red Jewels'
p73: Actinidia sinensis | Juncus spiralis | Malus | Zantedeschia 'Red Sox'

NATASHA LISITSA [USA]

p 74, 76: Betula papyrifera | Celastrus orbiculatus | Dahlia | Hippeastrum | Lilium 'Sumatra' | Oncidium (Chocolate) | Passiflora | Protea | Prunus | Punica granatum
Salix matsudana 'Tortuosa' | pheasant feathers (dyed fuchsia

p 77, 78: Dicranopteris linearis (Gleicheniaceae) | Gloriosa rothschildiana | Hippeastrum | Oncidium (Chocolate) | Paphiopedilum King Arthur cultivars | Passiflora |
Zantedeschia 'Majestic Red' | peacock feathers | pheasant feathers (dyed turquoise)

p 79a: Aeonium arboreum 'Zwartkop' | Allium sphaerocephalum | ostrich feather (dyed turquoise)
p 79b: Paphiopedilum | peacock feathers | pheasant feather (dyed turquoise)

p 80: Anemone | Dahlia | Dendrobium | Heliconia psittacorum | Manzanita (branch) | Mokara | Punica granatum | Zantedeschia
p 81: Dahlia | Gloriosa rothschildiana

Clematis vitalba | Dendrobium | Manzanita | Mokara | Pheasant feathers (dyed turquoise)

أحباء

RAYMOND CHOUITY [Saudi-Arabia]

p 84: Celosia cristata | Curcuma | Dracaena sanderiana | orchid sp. | Rosa sp.
p 86-87: Amaranthus caudatus | Eucalyptus | Hydrangea arborescens 'Annabelle' | Medinilla magnifica | Pyracantha | Rosa sp.

Amaranthus caudatus | Curcuma | Hydrangea arborescens 'Annabelle' | Rosa sp.

CLAIRE COWLING [United Kingdom]

p90: Vases: Alchemilla mollis | Astrantia | Ceropegia woodii | Chrysanthemum | Clematis | David Austin Rose 'Juliet & Miranda' | Eustoma grandiflora | Hebe | Matricaria | Nigella | Rosa 'Pepita' | Rosa 'Sweet Avalanche' | Stipa gigantean | Xanthorrhoea

Table: Alchemilla mollis | Astrantia | Ceropegia woodii | Chrysanthemum | David Austin Rose 'Juliet & Miranda' | Eustoma grandiflora | Hebe | Matricaria | Muehlenbeckia | Nigella | Papaver | Rosa 'Pepita' | Rosa 'Sweet Avalanche' | Rosa 'Wedding day' | Viburnum tinus

p92: Bridesmaid's wand: Ceropegia woodii | David Austin Rose: Juliet | Matricaria | Rosa 'Pepita' | Stachys byzantina

Bridal bouquet: Ceropegia woodii | Clematis | David Austin Rose 'Juliet & Miranda' | Hydrangea | Lunaria annua | Rosa 'Pepita' | Rosa 'Sweet Avalanche'

Bridesmaids posy: Clematis | David Austin Rose 'Juliet & Miranda' | Hydrangea | Lunaria annua | Matricaria | Rosa 'Pepita' | Rosa 'Sweet Avalanche'

Alchemilla mollis | Astrantia | Ceropegia woodii | Chrysanthemum | David Austin Rose 'Juliet & Miranda' | Eustoma grandiflora | Hebe | Matricaria | Muehlenbeckia | Nigella | Papaver | Rosa 'Pepita' | Rosa 'Sweet Avalanche' | Rosa 'Wedding day' | Viburnum tinus

p 96: Amaranthus caudatus | Dianthus caryophyllus | Ceropegia woodii | Chrysanthemum | Clematis | David Austin Rose 'Juliet & Miranda' |
Hebe | Rosa 'Pepita' | Rosa 'Sweet Avalanche' | Senecio rowleyanus | Viburnum tinus
p 97: Amaranthus caudatus | David Austin Rose 'Miranda' | Rosa 'Pepita' | Rosa 'Sweet Avalanche'

Alchemilla mollis | Amaranthus | Chrysanthemum | David Austin Rose 'Miranda & Juliet' | Dianthus | Eustoma Hebe | Panicum 'Fountain' | Rosa 'Sweet Avalanche' | Viburnum tinus

JOUNI SEPPÄNEN [Finland]

p100: Anacheilium crassilabium | Gastrochilus somai | Helianthus annuus 'Allegro' | Malleola baliensis | Rosa 'Rimini'
p102: **bouquet:** Anacheilium crassilabium | Gastrochilus somai | Helianthus annuus 'Allegro' | Malleola baliensis | Rosa 'Rimini' **roof:** Chrysanthemum 'Reagan Sunny' |
Gerbera 'Captiva' | Gerbera mini 'Banana' (Germini) | Gerbera mini 'Davidson' (Germini) | Helianthus annuus 'Allegro' | Helianthus annuus 'Little Leo'
p103: Anacheilium crassilabium | Gastrochilus somai | Helianthus annuus 'Allegro' | Malleola baliensis | Rosa 'Rimini'

p104: Anacheilium crassilabium | Gastrochilus somai | Helianthus annuus 'Allegro' | Malleola baliensis | Rosa 'Rimini'
p105: Helianthus annuus 'Allegro' | Hydrangea paniculata 'Mustila' | Rosa 'Rimini' | Zinnia elegans 'Lilleput Yellow'

p106: Chrysanthemum 'Reagan Sunny' | Helianthus annuus 'Allegro' | Helianthus annuus 'Little Leo' | Rosa 'Rimini'
p107: Chrysanthemum 'Reagan Sunny' | Gerbera 'Captiva' | Gerbera mini 'Banana' (Germini) | Gerbera mini 'Davidson' (Germini) |
Hedera helix 'Montgomery' | Helianthus annuus 'Allegro' | Helianthus annuus 'Little Leo' | Rosa 'Rimini'

DANIEL SANTAMARIA [Spain]

Asclepias 'Beatriz' | Gloriosa rotschildiana |
Phalaenopsis 'Detroit' | Xanthorrhoea australis |
Zantedeschia 'Schwarzwalder'

Ceropegia sandersonii | Gloriosa rotschildiana | Phalaenopsis 'Detroit' | Rosa rugosa (fruit) | Xanthorrhoea australis | Zantedeschia 'Schwarzwalder'

Altar: Asclepias 'Beatrix' | Gloriosa rotschildiana | Hedera helix | Hydrangea macrophylla | Malus crittendep | Rosa 'Red Mikado' | Rosa 'Ruby Red' |
Rosa rugosa (fruit) | Scabiosa stellata | Viburnum lantana
Pillars: Dianthus 'Sims' | Gladiolus sp | Gloriosa rotschildiana | Passiflora caerulea | Xanthorrhoea australis | Zantedeschia 'Schwartzwalder'

Asclepias 'Beatriz' | Gloriosa rotschildiana | Hydrangea macrophylla | Malus crittenden | Passiflora caerulea | Phalaenopsis 'Detroit' | Rosa 'Red Mikado' | Rosa 'Ruby Red' | Rosa rugosa (fruit) | Viburnum lantana | Xanthorrhoea australis

p 118: Asclepias 'Beatriz' | Gloriosa rotschildiana | Hydrangea macrophylla | Malus crittenden | Passiflora caerulea | Phalaenopsis 'Detroit' | Rosa 'Red Mikado' |
Rosa 'Ruby Red' | Rosa rugosa (fruit) | Viburnum lantana | Xanthorrhoea australis

p 119: Ceropegia sandersonia | Dianthus 'Sims' | Malus crittenden | Phalaenopsis 'Detroit' | Viburnum lantana | Xanthorrhoea australis

BRENDA LEE MONTEIRO [Singapore]

p120: Ceropegia | Gypsophila 'Million Stars' | Phalaenopsis
p122: Gypsophila 'Million Stars' | Phalaenopsis
p123: Gypsophila 'Million Stars' | Phalaenopsis | Ranunculus | Salix viminalis | orchid root

p124: Pillow: Gypsophila 'Million Stars' | Phalaenopsis | Allium sativum var. ophioscorodon
      Tie: Gypsophila 'Million Stars' | Phalaenopsis | orchid root
p125: Allium sativum var. ophioscorodon | Gypsophila 'Million Stars' | Phalaenopsis | orchid root

Allium sativum var. ophioscorodon | Gypsophila 'Million Stars' | Phalaenopsis | orchid root

p128: Bambusa (white) | Prunus serrulata | Rosa | orchid
foto: Kelvin Cuff
p129: Dianthus | Hydrangea | Phalaenopsis | Rosa sp |
Salix | Zantedeschia | moss

Jeg

elsker

deg

KRISTIN VORELAND [Norway]

Convallaria majalis | Gypsophilia paniculata | Ornithogalum dubium

Convallaria majalis | Gypsophilia paniculata | Ornithogalum dubium

Convallaria majalis | Gypsophilia paniculata | Ornithogalum dubium

Convallaria majalis | Gypsophilia paniculata | Ornithogalum dubium

ROBERT **KOENE**
(GREECE)

p 6 > 19

www.robertkoene.com

Robert graduated from the 'Huis te Lande College' in the Netherlands in 1987. In 1991 he earned his Master degree at the same college. From 1992 until 1994 Robert Koene worked in Japan as a floral designer and teacher. Robert kept traveling the world which eventually brought him to Saudi Arabia, where he worked for a long time and designed and coordinated the floral styling of no less than 18 royal weddings, large parties, official lunches and special events. In 2002 he won 4th place in the Dutch Flower Contest for Professionals and in the same year he attended the seminar for Competition Judges by the European Florist Association. He has been a judge for many floral competitions, is a sought after teacher and lecturer and continues to travel the globe to give demonstrations and workshops (AIFD, Hortifair Holland, Interflora Greece). Robert Koene has been living in Athens for over 10 years where he owns his own consulting company dealing with special events and floral decoration. He was a founder and teacher of the DFA program in Greece, the first institutionalized educational program in Greece. Robert Koene is specialized in custom designed weddings with a distinctive, own style. Robert is teaching in Greece as well as elsewhere in the world. Especially his wedding designs are highly desired and have been published in many international art books and specialized magazines such as *Fusion Flowers* (UK), *Bloem en Blad* (NL), *De Pook* (BE), *Flowers&* (US), *Fiori&Foglie* (IT) *Anthi kai Diakosmisi* (GR) to name a few.

Photography: Photis Karapiperis
www.studioverve.gr

Special thanks to: Location Island Club:
www.islandartandtaste.gr, www.panasgroup.gr
Flowers sponsored by Reneiri www.reineri.nl
and Dutch Creations www.dutch-creations.nl
My models Whitney, Emilie Lilga and my mini model
Eliana Koene

Wedding dress: Pronovias www.pronovias.gr
Styling: Anna Maria Barouh
Porto Elounda Hotel: www.elounda-sa.com
Assistants: Dimitris, Vassiliki, Despina and Rouli

ELENA **ANTIPINA**
(RUSSIA)

p 20 > 33

Elena Antipina was born in 1959 in the city of Vologda. She graduated from art school and pursued a career in pedagogy. Always fascinated by floristry, she followed her heart and took courses in floral art and craft with Ursula Wegener and Waltraud Maisch. Elena Antipina often participates in floral workshops in Russia and abroad. Always searching to perfect her skills, Elena traveled to Taiwan, where she studied with Ellie Lin. After taking courses and workshops in Belgium with Daniel Ost, she was invited to be a member of his team to decorate the temple in Japan (2007).

Her love for the homeland makes Elena not only participate in floral exhibitions but she also organizes and conducts them. She was one of the driving forces behind very successful exhibitions held in the Vologda State Historical-Architectural Museum-Reserve, the annual flower carnival in the Russian House (since 2005) and open-air exhibitions held in the Vologda Kremlin (2007-2009). The strongest aspect of Elena Antipina's skill is her feeling and connection with natural material, her ability to work with botanical materials, giving them a voice to evoke what is difficult to put down in words. In the featured wedding she translated the beauty of meadows, the blue sky above the city and the cold blue of the Vologda river into flowers. Russia has preserved many traditions and customs and Elena Antipina is a master in transferring this cultural heritage into floral art. Combining the ancient stories and techniques with modern technology results in distinctive, unusual work with a rare quiet beauty that leaves a very strong and lasting impression.

Photography: Vadim Shekun (Creative studio INTRO)

Special thanks to the models: Eldar Mamedov,
Katya Chashinova, Ksenia Uglova, Lilya Gogoleva,
Masha Sivkova, Oleg Efremov, Vasiliy Smirnov

MARK **PAMPLING**
(AUSTRALIA)

p 34 > 41

www.markpampling.com

At four years of age Mark Pampling won an art competition with a painting titled 'Grandma's Roses'. This was perhaps the start of his fascination with flowers and their artistic and creative possibilities. Almost twenty years later Mark abandoned painted flowers in favor of the real thing and has enjoyed exploring their design potential ever since. Competitive floristry has played an important role in his career, with successes in state and national competitions, and a third prize at the Interflora World Cup in 2004. Structured styles and clean lines have become familiar elements in his designing.

Mark calls Alstonville, in the lush north-eastern corner of New South Wales (Australia), his home, and enjoys teaching advanced floristry regularly at the local technical college. He also co-owns Alstonville Florist. Freelance designing has taken Mark all around Australia and the world, most recently workshops, lectures and demonstrations brought him to Japan, the Philippines, Thailand, Vietnam, New Zealand, the Netherlands, Germany, Canada and the USA. His designs have often been featured in the trendsetting magazines of the trade such as *Fusion Flowers* and *Fleur Creatief*.

Photography: Naomi Clarkson

THEA **KORNHERR**
(GERMANY)

p 42 > 55

www.kornherr.eu

Thea Kornherr (1978) grew up amidst the flowers in the garden design and flower business of her parents in Dettenhausen. She received her first training in floristics at Blumen Glemser (Stuttgart) and continued to study with Annette Kamping. Thea Kornherr strongly believes in taking part in floral competitions, something she did from a very young age. According to Kornherr it tremendously helps to grow as a florist, because people are most open-minded and receptive to ideas and influences at a young age. Besides that making mistakes in youth is easily forgiven. As the youngest competitor in the young florist's contest in Stuttgart she won an impressive sixth place. Two years later in 1997 she won the second place in the same competition. Her graduation project earned her a scholarship, used for a six month study with the famous Elly Lin in Taiwan. Thea Kornherr took master classes and workshops with Gregor Lersch, Ursula Wegener, Olaf Schroers and many other German masters. She represented Germany at the Montreal Florist Cup in 2000 and in 2004 and won second place at the prestigious Silver Rose competition in Baden-Württemberg. From 1995 until 2000 she was the assistant of many master florists in Germany and abroad amongst whom Nicole von Boletzky, Wally Klett and Tor Gundersen. Her designs always start from the material itself; what are its possibilities and what are the limitations? This avoids stepping into the pitfall of having some archetypical designs and shapes and just replacing the flowers in them. Keeping an open mind is key. Thea's work is often featured in *Florieren!*, she gives lectures, demonstrations and workshops around Germany and Europe and at the same time still continues to work at the family business in Dettinghausen.

Photography: Gaby Höss

GARY **KWOK**
(HONG KONG)

p 56 > 67

www.garykwok.com

Gary Kwok is one of the pioneers in the competitive Hong Kong floral arena. Gary is the founder of Gary K Limited, with her outstanding achievement in creative floral arrangements, Gary K Limited has made its quick ascent towards the leading and trendsetting business it is now. From 2005 it has become the most applauded company in event decoration and weddings of prestige. Gary studied floral arrangements in Japan (Miyuki Art Flower Studio), Paris (École Française de Décoration Florale), Belgium (Daniel Ost) and at the three famous British institutes for floral design: the Constance Spry Flower School, Jane Packer Flower School and Paula Pryke Flower School. Amongst all the various floral styles she acquired over the years, it was the Japanese art of Ikebana that initially sparked her interest in flowers. Gary's passion and innovation in floral design has earned her a list of devoted international clienteles, which include both celebrity clients, big names in fashion and luxury brands such as Armani, Burberry, Cartier, Louis Vuitton, Yves Saint Laurent and many more. Floral arrangements designed by Gary are often inspired and influenced by interior designs, architecture and fashion. She is a well sought after decorator for hotels and big events. Her floral arrangements demonstrate a new use of form, color and texture and integrate both the flowers and the vase, creating a clean and modern look.

Photography: William Lygratte and Chris Chan

GIORDANO **SIMONELLI**
(ITALY)

p 68 > 73

www.giordanosimonelli.it

Giordano Simonelli is a well established name in the Italian floral scene and especially in his home town of Castelnovo ne' Monti, where he has been a florist since 1966. After receiving his first education in floral design at Federfiori, he perfected his skills taking workshops around Europe and an internship at FEUPF in Grünberg (Germany). In 1990 he represented Italy at Hortiflora in Paris, where he was the one responsible for the team's vision and philosophy of only working with natural elements and taking advantage of natural lines and shapes in materials without too much designer's intervention. Since 1985 he was appointed teacher at Federfiori, where he brought new inspiration and new courses, and upgraded and lifted many of the basic courses to a higher plan. At Federfiori he held technical and organizational tasks of various kinds, he was jointly responsible for the coordination of the Europe Cup team in 1999, he was in charge of the technical field related to publishing and a member of the coordinating committee of the San Remo flower market. He was presenter and commentator for the Europe Cup, five Italian cups and other major events in the floral industry. Giordano Simonelli won numerous competitions around Italy and Europe, he also worked for television, was the editorial director for the magazine *Flowers*, which was revived under his guidance, and author of a publication on funeral design.

Photography: James Bragazzi

NATASHA **LISITSA**
(USA)

p 74 > 83

www.waterlilypond.com

Natasha Lisitsa, owner and lead designer of Waterlily Pond Floral and Event Design Studio in San Francisco, has become widely recognized for her exuberant style and innovative use of plant materials.

Natasha worked as an engineer before leaving the high-tech industry to pursue her love of flowers and art. She studied floral design at the Sogetsu School of Ikebana and developed her own style fusing Eastern and Western design principles, often referred to as 'exuberant Ikebana'. She founded Waterlily Pond Studio in 2001 and grew it into one of the most sought-after sources for weddings and special events in the San Francisco Bay Area. In 2008, Waterlily Pond was voted 'Best of the Bay Wedding Flowers' by *San Francisco Chronicle readers*.

Natasha has been commissioned by the San Francisco Museum of Modern Art, the de Young Museum and other prominent cultural organizations to create large-scale floral art installations. Natasha's work has been published in international and U.S. publications, including *Fusion Flowers, Flower, Martha Stewart Weddings, People, The Knot Weddings, Brides, Grace Ormonde Wedding Style,* and many more.

Natasha is also an accomplished lecturer-demonstrator of floral art. Recent presentations include an exciting 1.5 hour program at the de Young Museum's Bouquets to Art exhibition in 2010, which earned a standing ovation from the assembled crowd of 300. A new program featuring large-scale floral sculptures will be presented at the prestigious AIFD (American Institute of Floral Designers) National Symposium in July 2011.

———

Photography: Erin Beach

RAYMOND **CHOUITY**
(SAUDI ARABIA)

p 84 > 89

Self-taught artist Raymond Chouity was discovered by Anais Nin in the early 1970's. Working quietly behind the scenes in the royal palaces of Saudi Arabia for over 25 years, Raymond Chouity and Salim Younes, respectively artistic director and owner of *Desert Rose*, have taken the commercial activity of their company from a small time supplier of floral arrangements to the royal family to Saudi Arabia's foremost concern in the event managements sector. None of this would have been possible without Raymond's commitment to innovative designs and the highest standards of production which have earned him the loyal support of the most influential hostesses in the Kingdom. Every client is unique and not two of his wedding designs will ever be the same, even though they are often staged in the same banqueting halls and palaces. Handpicked flowers and a selection of rich and luxury accessories play an unforgettable role on the stage that is Raymond's creative genius come to dramatic life. Raymond Chouity captures the unique personality and preferences of his brides; a quality that has endeared him to the Saudi royal family for two successive generations. Raymond's extraordinary designs for diplomatic dinners, royal honeymoons, VIP parties, celebrity proposals have been preserved for eternity in a stunning coffee table book published by his friend and publisher Hani J. Samaha.

———

Special thanks to: Hani J. Samaha
www.samahabooks.com

CLAIRE **COWLING**
(UNITED KINGDOM)

p 90 > 99

www.thrivefloristry.com

Claire Cowling's natural creativity and flair for design was born when working in the family floristry shop. She developed her skills and experience in the shop and her own workshop whilst studying for formal floristry qualifications. Claire's experience and reputation continued to flourish and she was soon invited to compete, exhibit and demonstrate at increasingly prestigious shows. Claire Cowling is now internationally recognised as one of the UK's leading florists. Her work frequently appears in competitive floristry books and in the national press. Claire is often a part of major international events, won numerous awards and prizes for her work and is co-author of several best-selling books *(Straight from the Heart* series, *Wedding bouquets for Spring)* and magazines *(Flowers for Funerals)* that other professional florists use for inspiration. Claire was instrumental in setting up and running *Thrive Floristry*, a specialist supplier of books and sundries for professionals. Next to this Claire travels across the UK and internationally to exhibit at shows, deliver sought-after tuition or provide consultation at leading events. Claire is renowned for her passion and perfectionism, especially for the Big Day. From buttonholes to bouquets, every detail of her work is carefully considered and beautifully constructed. With a wealth of experience in weddings and events, Claire sets the standard in beautiful floral wedding design — literally. She has written and published several industry books and magazines for professional florists to use with their clients.

———

Photography: Bruce Head
Special thanks to the sponsors: Smithers
Oasis UK, David Austin Roses

JOUNI **SEPPÄNEN**
(FINLAND)

p100 > 107

www.jouniseppanen.com

Jouni Seppänen's life has always evolved around nature and flowers. Born in 1961 in the beautiful surroundings of Kangasniemi it was easy to be taken in by nature's splendor. His love of animals and all things living destined him to become a veterinarian. While other boys were obsessed by cars and motors, Jouni found himself reading nature guides and learning the scientific names of the local flora and fauna. But when one day he journeyed into the flower shop of his village, all ideas of becoming a veterinarian left him and were replaced by a new dream. Obsessed by the newfound passion, he was quickly fully immersed in the world of floristry and floral art. There was no turning back. In 1984 Jouni graduated as a florist and that same year he became the Finnish national champion. A honor that would be given to him many more times (1985, '89, '90, '99 and 2000). After earning his teacher's degree (1985) he pursued his career further and took the master degree in floristry and horticulture (1992-2002). In 2008 he was voted President of the Finnish Florist's Association. Jouni Seppänen is a frequent competitor in many competitions both in Scandinavia and in the rest of Europe, often winning or earning a lot of honorary places. In 2010 he was the Finnish contestant in the Interflora World Cup Competition in Shanghai. Jouni Seppänen still travels the world to learn, to share his knowledge and to inspire people.

Photography: Jouni Seppänen

DANIEL **SANTAMARÍA I PUEYO**
(SPAIN)

p108 > 119

www.floristik-projekt.com

Daniel Santamaría I Peuyo is Master Florist at the Escola d'Art Floral de Catalunya, acknowledged by the FEEF. He completed his teacher's training courses at the Generalitat de Catalunya and perfected his art during specialized courses with master florists such as Benedicto Llum I Alonso, Montserrat Bolet, Gregor Lersch, Wally Klett, Nicole von Boletzky and many others. Together with Brigitta Ohlrogge he teaches pedagogy courses for floral art teachers in Hamburg and at the Escola d'Art Floral, where he has been a teacher since 1997. Daniel Santamaría teaches and gives lectures and workshops in different training centers throughout Spain, Europe, Latin America and Asia. He realizes exhibitions and floral art demonstrations in companies and entities in the floral sector, both national and international. He was champion of the Catalunya Floral Art Cup (1996) and of the Spanish Floral Art Cup (1997) and runner-up in the European Floral Art Cup in 2003. In 2005 he assisted in the Spanish Floral Art cup. Since 2003 he owns his own company Floristik Projekt in Hamburg and since 2009 he is the artistic director and coordinator of the Escola d'Art Floral de Catalunya.

Floral works: Daniel Santamaría and Britta Ohlrogge

Photography: Guillem Urbá

In collaboration with: Uxua Cierbide Górriz, Jorge Clemos Manrique, José Ángel Colmenero Hernández, Marta Diego Díez, Ricardo Enerziz Arriazu, Ainara Ezpeleta Gago, Marta Fernández Rebolé, Maite García Elizalde, Margarita Garralda Larumbe, Arantza Ibañez Echazarreta, Esther Irigoyen Otazu, Maia Morrás del Río, Juan Carlos Martínez Parra, Maria Teresa Miramón Alonso, Maite Soria Martinez, Julia Vicondoa Etcheverry

Special thanks to the sponsors: Oasis Spain, ASVnatur, Nasoflor, Escola d'Art Floral de Catalunya, Carmen Ibanez Ursúa, Texflors, City council Tiebas

BRENDA LEE **MONTEIRO**
(SINGAPORE)

p120 > 129

www.fioredorato.com.sg

If you'd ask Brenda Lee Monteiro if flowers were her first passion, she will admit in all honesty that she was never a flower child. Yet today her passion for flowers has become an inseparable part of her life. Her love of creation and all things beautiful led her to a study in fashion. But as soon as she found out that floral design allowed her the same visual gratification as the fashion industry, what had started out as a hobby soon was carving her career path. She headed to Holland, Belgium, Paris, San Francisco, Hong Kong and many more places where she could experience floral artistry in action and learn from the best. In May 2001 she got her Master's degree in Floral Design, the next year she was introduced into the American Institute of Floral Designers (AIFD). Brenda Lee Monteiro has a very personal vision on floral art and aspires to change the mindset of many people believing that flowers are nothing but accessories. People should embrace flowers for their beauty and personality. In 1996 her own floral boutique 'Fiore Dorato' ('Golden Flowers') opened the doors. As the name of her shop suggest quality and exquisite flower arrangements have been the main focus. Brenda Lee has conceptualized and realized a great number of lavish weddings and she has long been recognized as one of the best florists in Singapore, earning her the *Singapore Tatler* award for Best Florist in Singapore for five consecutive years. With 15 years of practical experience, Brenda is an excellent teacher and desires to share her design expertise and creative philosophy with every person wanting to be equipped with the necessary skills, be it for professional reasons or personal enrichment.

Photography: Jayce Goh, 39 East Photography, Kelvin Cuff

KRISTIN VORELAND
(NORWAY)

p 130 > 139

www.atelierflora.no

Kristin Voreland has been passionate about flowers all her life. She studied at the Beder Gartnerskole in Denmark and received her professional floral training in Norway, Denmark and Belgium. She took additional specialization courses at the Art Academy of Bergen (Norway) and won several gold and silver medals, both in regional, national and international competitions. She was European Champion in 1986 and won the Norwegian Championship in 1987. Together with her team she also won the Scandinavian Cup in 1989. The Floristic Craft Award, the most prestigious award in the field of floral design in Norway, was awarded to her in 2003. She frequently holds seminars, master classes and exhibitions, which brought her to 25 different countries, and has been a distinguished member of the jury at several national and international competitions in floral design. One of Kristin's favorite aspects of the profession is exhibiting her work in art galleries, which she had been doing almost every year, several of them abroad and on invitation of galleries. For over 25 years Kristin Voreland has successfully been running Atelier Flora. No standard work is to be found in her shop, her company has a very personal touch and creates everything from common bouquets to extraordinary 12 meter tall decorated steel Christmas trees for hotels and business environments. Kristin's shop has its own welding department, which allows her to design monumental pieces in which botanical materials can be used in extraordinary ways. No challenge is too big for Kristin and her team.

Photography: Påll Hoff
Dress design: Anne Lise Tollefsen
Special thanks to: Katrine V. Hestholm and her horse Jesper

CONCEPT
Jaak Van Damme

ARTISTS
Brenda Lee Monteiro (Singapore)
Claire Cowling (United Kingdom)
Daniel Santamaria I Pueyo (Spain)
Elena Antipina (Russia)
Gary Kwok (Hong Kong)
Giordano Simonelli (Italy)
Jouni Seppänen (Finland)
Kristin Voreland (Norway)
Mark Pampling (Australia)
Natasha Lisitsa (USA)
Raymond Chouity (Saudi Arabia)
Robert Koene (Greece)
Thea Kornherr (Germany)

LAY-OUT
www.groupvandamme.eu

PRINT
www.pureprint.be

FINAL EDITING
Katrien Van Moerbeke

PUBLISHED BY
Stichting Kunstboek bvba
Legeweg 165
B-8020 Oostkamp
T. +32 50 46 19 10
F. +32 50 46 19 18
info@stichtingkunstboek.com
www.stichtingkunstboek.com

ISBN 978-90-5856-330-9
D/2011/6407/11
NUR 421

© Stichting Kunstboek, 2011

George Herriman asleep at his drawing board in the art room of the *New York Evening Journal*, c. 1916, with a *Baron Bean* strip in progress. Originally published in *The Comic Art of George Herriman*. Special thanks to the co-editor of that invaluable book, Patrick McDonnell, for letting us use it here, and to Josepe Gaignard at www.coconino-world.com for additional retouching and period-style duotoning.

⊗. KRAZY & IGNATZ. ⚡.

by George Herriman.

"A Kind, Benevolent and Amiable Brick."

Convening the Full-Page Comic Strips.

1919-1921.

Edited by Bill Blackbeard
With an introduction by Bob Callahan

Fantagraphics Books, SEATTLE.

Krazy Kat By Her

Published by Fantagraphics Books.
7563 Lake City Way North East,
Seattle, Washington, 98115, United States of America.

Edited by Bill Blackbeard.
Except where noted, all research materials appear courtesy of the San Francisco Academy of Cartoon Art.
Cover & endpapers design by Chris Ware.
Interior design by Alexa Koenings, based on a template by Chris Ware.
Production assistance and scanning by Paul Baresh.
Eric Reynolds, Associate Publisher.
Published by Gary Groth and Kim Thompson.
Krazy & Ignatz — A Kind, Benevolent and Amiable Brick is copyrighted © 2011 Fantagraphics Books.
All rights reserved. Permission to reproduce material from this book, except for purposes of review and/
or notice, must be obtained from the publisher. For a free full-color catalogue of comics and cartooning,
including many classic American newspaper strips, please telephone 1-800-657-1100.
Our books may be viewed and purchased by consulting www.fantagraphics.com on your home terminal.

First Fantagraphics Books edition: January 2011.

ISBN: 978-1-60699-364-4.

Printed in Korea through Print Vision.

Special thanks to Derya Ataker, Jeet Heer, Dean Mullaney and Cat Yronwode, and Michael Tisserand.

riman ⊗. **KRAZY & IGNATZ.** ⚡.

A MOUSE BY ANY NAME:

KRAZY AND IGNATZ'S EARLY LIFE UNDER THE BOARDS

by Bill Blackbeard

It all began with a kat and a mouse, and occasionally a bulldog and a duck. Their little four- or five-panel encounters, often wordless, found at the foot of the *Dingbat Family* and *Family Upstairs* strips from 1910 to 1914, existed at first chiefly to give their creator, George Herriman of the *New York Evening Journal*, an amusing way to kill what remained of his eight-hour office stint at the paper after he had finished his work on the day's parent strip. Names they had nix. The kat herself had acquired a public name through general appreciation of the mouse character's early, hurled insult, "krazy kat!" (preceded a day or so earlier by a less catchy "fool kat!"), which Herriman himself liked and repeated via the mouse from time to time through the early months of the strip. But the mouse who was to be Ignatz went on as nameless, except for such passing appellations as "you," "mouse," "Mr. Mouse," and (in an odd moment of unmerited respect) "sir" bestowed upon him by the "krazy kat," and the similarly unnamed duck and bulldog. None of this was surprising. The

early antics of this animal cast were funny but rudimentary, and names would have seemed a wholly uncalled-for embellishment. And yet, as the delighted public feedback on the Herriman critters grew through the summer of 1910, the artist finally gave the kat's crew their own set of downstairs panels, away from the family into which they had been born upstairs. Here they flourished; dialogue balloons spread to encompass the same kind of Herriman poesy regularly uttered at grand comic length by the Dingbats. Tenuous characters were now firmed into familiar figures. The readers grew more appreciative, and it was clear to the thin man at the *Family Upstairs* drawing board that it was time to name, and begin to provide background information on, his new four-footed crowd. At the end of 1910, in two remarkable daily episodes of *The Family Upstairs*, Herriman opened the floodgates not only on new and hitherto unrecorded data about his Dingbat ménage and their residential obsession, but also upon the wholly engrossing backgrounds of the finally named Krazy

FACING PAGE: *Herriman's first Ignatz, as shown in this October 8, 1910 installment of* The Family Upstairs, *was an Irish janitor, Ignatz O'Brien.*

THIS PAGE: *Two and a half months later, in the December 30, 1910 strip, Herriman bequeathed the name to Ignatz Mouse, and history was made.*

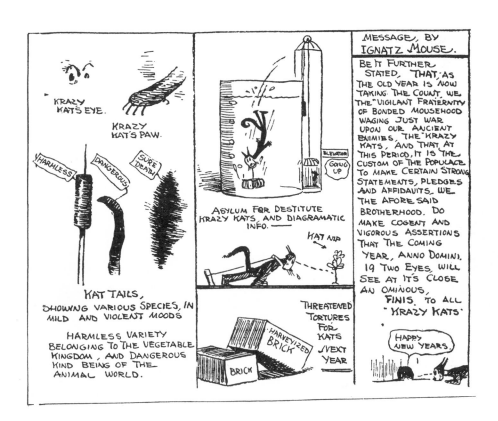

Typical episodes (April 7, 1914; January 14, 1915; June 2, 1915) of The Dingbat Family *after the family downstairs had vacated its footer compartment, and gone off to form its own new strip, a curious number called* Krazy Kat.

Kat and Ignatz Mouse themselves, much of it, in the expected Herriman touch, preposterously irrelevant. (The duck, who in full nomenclatural regalia would be Gooseberry Sprigg, the Duke Duck, and the bulldog whose future lay with the Coconino constabulary, were omitted from this king-sized exposé. They would develop speedily enough in the strip itself.)

Meanwhile, more than likely sensing that the kat and mouse team would eventually have a bright future on their own, but biding his time as a desk-bound, eight-to-five Hearst employee assigned major work on another strip, Herriman continued to work zest and imagination on the bizarrely-conceived *The Family Upstairs* through the next year and a half. Reflecting the freshly odd aspects of "flat" or apartment living just being encountered by tens of thousands of city-dwelling, office-working

American families, the Dingbats were first irritated by their noisy, party-giving, obviously exotic — but maddeningly unseen and unreachable — upstairs neighbors. The variations wrought by Herriman on this engaging but seemingly simple theme over more than fifteen months — raids and attacks on the obtuse neighbors by balloon, airplane, cannon, flood, plagues and fire on the one hand, and by hired detectives, hypnotists, magicians, wrestlers, burglars and showgirls on the other — has to be read to be believed. And relished.

Before the *Family Upstairs* epic ran its course, however, between August 1, 1910 and November 15, 1911, Herriman created still another brilliant, short-lived introductory strip called *The Dingbat Family*. Begun before *The Family Upstairs*, and suspended during the Family's reign, Herriman returned to his beloved Dingbats after the great interfamilial siege ended, continuing *The Dingbat Family* until its cast took a final bow on January 4, 1916. In the meantime, the independent daily *Krazy Kat* strip Herriman had anticipated began on October 28, 1913, running on the *New York Journal* comic page in a vertical, page-high stack of five tall panels beside the horizontal rows of regularly laid-out comics — including The *Dingbat Family*, finally bereft of its raucous animal cast. The Kat's congeries of big city fans applauded the move, and the new strip began what was to be an unbroken run in a number of Hearst papers from 1913 until Herriman's death in 1944 — a blithe and peaceful history in contrast to the a traumatic career of the *Kat* Sunday pages collected in these volumes. (But then, a single daily strip lost on a page containing from ten to thirty other strips can, in the editorial view, be permitted eccentricities forbidden to a full, highly visible, and costly Sunday comic page.)

The Dingbats' funky career ended in midweek in January, 1916. The next day, January 5, 1916, Herriman introduced the Chaplinesque star of his new daily strip, *Baron Bean*. *Baron Bean* was to be Herriman's last major daily strip — the odd, oversized *Stumble Inn* of the early 1920s was basically ancillary to the Sunday page of the same name, and ran only a few months — and it was something of a masterpiece along the comic lines of *Don Quixote*, *Sir Launcelot Greaves*, and *The Pickwick Papers*.

The good Baron — whose actual first name was as elusive as that of Herriman's mouse at the outset of the *Family Upstairs* strip — was a transparent con man basically capable of deluding no one other than himself, and his devoted man servant, the loyal, cynical yet insightful

C. Cephus Grimes. The financial needs of this new team was the narrative goad of the new strip, and for the next three years Herriman extracted reams of splendid comedy and fantasy from it — until the strip's conclusion on January 10, 1919.

The decade of the 1910s, which saw the launching of three important Herriman dailies, as well as the daily and Sunday *Krazy Kat* page, was probably the most productive decade of the cartoonist's busy career, and certainly among the richest in inspiration and accomplishment. These pages form a too-brief graphic summary of the daily strip work of that period, but as the wind witches of Wunanji might croon in their breezy wisdom — appetites whetted may one day be sated, if our readers bear with us. And try to duck the bricks of the laggardly named Ignatz Mouse, the rowdy, pestiferous, mean, ornery, and let's face it — altogether superb, underlying star of these pages.

Typical episodes (May 8 and May 9, 1916) of Baron Bean, *dealing with the relationship between the Baron and his manservant, C. Cephus Grimes. Note the name of Graimes's non-defunct uncle: Ignacio Ratón.*

GEO. HERRIMAN'S LOS ANGELES

by Bob Callahan

Some odd, goofy new blend of surrealism, American style, was born in the City of Angels back in 1906 when the future creator of *Krazy Kat,* George Herriman, a Creole gentleman from awl N'awlins, picked up a number of his very best pencils and began to sketch offbeat human interest stories for the pages of the *Los Angeles Times.*

Keaton at Burbank, Jelly Roll at Jass City, and Herriman at the *Times* — it was Dawn, and the song was called Ragtime. Pregnant with possibilities, a new American century was about to be born.

We must thank the Gods responsible for human laughter that Herriman was given the opportunity to create this new body of work, for at the time, dear George's newspaper career was already pretty much on the skids. Herriman had in fact been booted from the sports department at the *New York American* only a few months before by a certain Mr. Julian Hawthorne, the grandson of the man who had written *The Scarlet Letter*, and easily the most boring sports editor ever to edit a sports department at the offices of a major American daily.

Prior to the arrival of the awful Hawthorne, Herriman had spent his time turning out wonderful sports cartoons for William Randolph Hearst while hanging out in local bars with the likes of Tad Dorgan, Hype Igoe, Rubber Nose Tom McNamara — an assorted gang of pre-Runyon Broadway types who, collectively, chose to give the mere notion of moderate behavior an early and very bad name. Indeed, Herriman was in mild danger of becoming a regular Broadway dandy himself when young Hawthorne came along, removed him from the sports page without a trace, and began to fill the section instead with his own tyrannical pontifications

about the virtues of physical culture. It is today easier to watch paint dry than it is to read Julian Hawthorne on the virtues of physical culture. Under Hawthorne's short but unhappy reign — heresy of heresies — the *American* even stopped running the daily ball scores for a while.

And so, in 1906, George Herriman limped across the continent to his adopted Los Angeles. and the Angels alone know what he would have done had not the editors of the *Times* shown the foresight to give him new work, and give it to him soon. Within months after his return to the city in which he had been raised after his family's move from Louisiana, Herriman was assigned a series of off-beat human interest stories, bizarre stories of small but interesting historical consequence filled with the kind of haunting details that always did manage to switch the pilot light on up in George's main cabin.

Before he could even mumble "Scarlet Letter," George Herriman was aswim in early Los Angeles popular culture, covering incidents ranging from the fate of a haunted Chinese boxer, to the first sightings of unidentified flying objects, to bull fights in nearby Tia Juana, to the capture of two of the old west's last highwaymen on the outskirts of San Bernardino. George Herriman's early Los Angeles newspaper art remains to this day a rare and welcome tribute to a profession — American journalism — which, in the early years of this century at least, didn't automatically put people to sleep with the sheer sameness of the drone. Herriman and his pals were firecrackers. As the old timers say, we are not liable to see their likes again.

Bums No Longer Brake at Newhall

NO MORE WILL PRISON WALLS GO UP IN SMOKE NEW
CEMENT LOCK-UP HARBINGER OF HARD TIMES HOBOS MUST
NOW SKIRT TOWN TO ESCAPE NEW CALABOOSE

One of George Herriman's earliest *Times* assignments was the opening of a new "bum's" jail out in Newhall. The business of opening new jails was at the time widely considered a tough-fisted civic response to the dozens — if not hundreds — of hobo camps and hobo orchards then spread across the County of Los Angeles. As the authorities imagined it, these new jails marked an end to an era — an era of "railroad-tie bonfires and tomato-can kitchens where weary vagrants find small relief from the smell of oil smoke in their lungs, and from the jolt of springless trucks in their bones."

These new jails, moreover, were relatively escape-proof, a major improvement over the series of wooden shacks the County had constructed in the past. The vagrants simply loved those old wooden shacks. In the old days, when anyone decided it was time to leave, he or she merely built a fire on the floor, waited for a wall to burn in, and then skipped off into the nearby desert. Sometimes the walls to these shacks were so skimpy, a fire wasn't even necessary. The hobos just escaped through the open holes. Finally the authorities moved in, and began to build the new cement slammers. Newhall was the prototype, constructed out of cement with walls twelve inches thick, and with cell windows opening only into an interior, well-secured courtyard, allowing escaping prisoners to get only so far as the nearest community sink. "Bums No Longer Brake At Newhall," the headline read. Whenever possible, the story stated, the hobos will now take the "A" train straight through to San Diego. Sitting at the edge of the desert, Newhall Jail haunted Herriman — whose sympathies were clearly with the vagrants. Years later a jail of similar exterior design would emerge in the middle of *Krazy Kat*. In time, this later "Newhall" would become the permanent home for Officer Pupp; from time to time, it would also serve as a regular hotel for both Ignatz and Krazy.

He-Cow Fighting as Tame as Ping Pong

SAD-EYED BOVINE SLAVERS RIDICULED ARTIST
NAMES BULL AS FORMER NEIGHBOR ILLUSTRATOR
HERRIMAN'S FIRST TRIP TO TIA JUANA

In the Summer of 1906, the *Los Angeles Times* sent George Herriman to Tia Juana, Mexico, to witness his first bullfight. At the time, a couple of Texas confidence men were trying to build a new bullfight market among the gringos in southern California.

The L.A. press, however, was less than sympathetic. Starting and ending with Herriman, the team from the *Times* loathed the very idea. The Tia Juana dispatches were loaded with both sarcasm and irony.

"Mr. Herriman is now in mourning," the paper carefully noted on its sports page. "He insists that the first wild, raging bull killed at Tia Juana this past Sunday was a close associate and playmate of his youth.

"He openly claims that he can still distinctly remember a time when that kind-faced old he-cow used to come around to the kitchen door and eat potato peelings directly out of his own baby hand.

"He further states that the proprietors of these matches will just have to realize that what might be taken as coldness on his part toward their so-called art is in fact simply the grief he is experiencing at this violent final parting with an old family pet."

The *Times* had little patience with the fight's opening ceremony. "First two dingy looking cow punchers in tinsel ride out on horseback and salute the provincial Governor," the *Times* reported. "Then, after the spectators recover, the gate of the bull pen opens, and the procession of toreadors enter the arena. The band then strikes up a gay and triumphant march which, while somewhat out of tune, is nonetheless meant to be very friendly. Finally the toreadors stand before the Governor, and say something bold and ceremonious to him in Spanish.

"Although he admits his own Spanish is rather weak, Mr. Herriman has translated the remarks to mean, roughly: 'I and my desperate friends will now try to make money waving rags at this genial old cow.'"

PERHAPS IT MAY
EXPLAIN WHY SO
MANY GREEN
MONGOLIANS ARE
WITH US JUST NOW.

UFO Sightings Haunt Imperial Valley

ALL IMPERIAL VALLEY AWED BY MONSTER THAT SOARS THROUGH
AIR MAKES QUEER CLICKING NOISE AND CARRIES A LIGHT
SHOULD SALT BE PUT ON TAIL OF THIS FLY BY NIGHT?

On the evening of May 30, 1906, Herriman went out to Imperial Valley to look into claims concerning the existence of an unidentified flying object which seemed to be driving local residents, and not a few itinerant cows, right to the edge of drink.

At a small farm outside the desert community of Brawley, a man by the name of Dagnall told Herriman that the UFO had first appeared to him some two months before. Back in June, Dagnall first heard the curious clickity-clickitying sound — a sound much like that of a small motor — through the stillness of a summer desert night. The object even passed his house, but Dagnall heard no more of it that first night.

The next night it came back again. This time Dagnall not only heard the sound, he also observed a queer light waving and bobbing through the clouds. Finally, in a great flash, the light bobbed out of sight, as if swallowed up in the darkness of the desert night sky.

For a long time Dagnall alone heard this odd, new nighttime sound. Then, about a month later, Mrs. Dagnall heard the sound too. She was too terrified to hang around and see anything, however. As the sound intensified, she came running back into the house, frightened and pale.

At this point, Mr. Dagnall told the *L.A. Times*, he became determined not to be haunted by this "thing" any longer. Just a few nights later, he finally took his long 45-70 Winchester rifle off the wall of his house; with a couple of local ranchers, he led a shooting party out to a clearing where they all waited in silence for the nightly over-flight.

After a considerable wait, Dagnall and his shooting party finally heard the now familiar clickity-click again. Indeed, they were just about to fire off a few thousand idle rounds when it suddenly occurred to Dagnall: What if this damn thing carries dynamite bombs? What if it's one of these new flying

machines being operated by either cattle rustlers, or people carrying alien Chinese over the Mexican border?

"Hold your fire, boys," Dagnall told his assembled militia, "I don't think we want to be chiefly responsible for the first synchronized bombing of the whole of Imperial Valley."

No, they did not.

Herriman returned to Los Angeles, dutifully impressed.

Within months after his return, Herriman was assigned a series of off-beat human interest stories, bizarre stories of small but interesting historical consequence filled with the kind of haunting details that always did manage to switch the pilot light on up in George's main cabin.

Splattered City in Middle of Sign Spat

RIVAL PAINTERS REALIZE ACUTE STATE OF FRIGHT
SLICK TRICKS ADOPTED BY ONE WORRIES ANOTHER
ENERGIES SCATTERED UNTIL LAW DECIDES POINT

Earlier in the year, Herriman had been assigned to cover a "splatter war" that had broken out on the streets of Los Angeles between two rival sign painters. "The town is awash in colors," the *Times* reported on Thursday, May 17, 1906. "Rival sign painters and angry billboard men are sloshing red, blue, green, yellow, purple and pink over every blank wall in the downtown area in a bitter war for painterly supremacy.

"Just to see who is who," the *Times* continued, "the painters will cross brushes in the Superior Court in a few days. In the meantime, in the face of dueling injunctions, the rival painters are scooting around the alleys, covering fences and other things with glaring statements for Dr. Dosem's Dental Floss, and for somebody's elses hot stuff for cold nights. While good people of aesthetic tastes are taking up the cudgels for a city beautiful, for sweeping views of the far-off mountains, these sign men are spilling paint around as recklessly as a stage actress trying to get on stage."

The trouble began when a certain Mr. Varney and a certain Mr. Green, both of San Francisco, decided it was time to do a little outdoor publicity business in the southern realms of the state. When they arrived in Los Angeles, Varney &. Green soon found that the leases on most of the important wall space were already opened by Mr. Ed Herwick, a local painter. Herwick, moreover, had no intention of cutting Varney & Green in on the business.

The San Francisco men soon found out that Herwick had signed most of his leases with the tenants of the buildings in question. They countered by signing counter-leases with many of the building's owners. Throughout Los Angles, Verney and Green began to paint over Mr. Herwick's signs — or the signs that he had rented out to his advertiser clients.

The war, of course, was on.

WHEN RIVAL ARTISTS MEET.

Mr. Herwick responded by painting over the Varney & Green repainting of his own original signs. Then Varney & Green returned, and began painting over the signs Herwick had painted over the signs that Varney & Green had painted over the original Herwicks in the first place. This was nuts, of course; and the pattern was being repeated all over town. As a personal contribution to the "splatter wars," which never really did get resolved, George Herriman was only too happy to add a few new illustrated cartoons of his own.

WING'S FIRST LESSON

World's First Chinese Boxer Visits Los Angeles

LOCAL CHINESE LOOK IN DISDAIN ON TINY AH WING
SISTERS WAIT IN VAIN FOR LETTER HE WILL NEVER WRITE
HE HATES IT, TOO, BUT DESTINY MADE HIM A PUG

On June 24, 1906, Herriman was assigned to cover the sad story of troubled Ah Wing, allegedly the world's only professional Chinese prize fighter. Born in Auburn, California, Wing was making his Los Angeles ring debut when he was profiled by the artist. As Herriman would soon learn, the local Chinese community had greeted the appearance of Ah Wing with scorn. "Only two Chinese men attended the fight" the newspaper reported. "Ah Wing's people have turned against him in silent disgust."

Wing, however, was not surprised. "No, they no come," he told the *Times*. "China boys no time for me. If they do come, they bet against me. They no like me for to prize fight. My people no like either."

Why had Ah Wing chosen this line of employment in the first place, the Times wondered? "No helping it," the boxer said.

"I went to a big school in Auburn where I was born. They just two China boys; one thousand white children. The white boys, they pick on us all the time and call names. Had to fight. I lick them all."

One day Ah Wing was walking down the street in Auburn, and a local businessman invited him to come over to the local athletic club just for a lark. "No gloves ever on my hands before," Ah Wing recalled. "No understand guard, no understand swing, punch. No understand anything. I walk up and hit the other man, and knock him clear through the window. Last year I make $2000. I got two sisters which I take care of. They not like me to fight. I tell them I write them a letter if I win tonight."

Unfortunately, Ah Wing's sisters would to have to keep waiting for that letter. In his Los Angeles debut, the 112-pound Chinese fighter was clearly out-muscled and outboxed by a local 133-pounder by the name of "Kid Williams." Wing was still bleeding in one eye, and his entire face was swollen when he talked to the press after the five-round bout. Somehow, he had at least preserved his sense of humor.

Wing was asked how far he generally ran each day during his road work. "Oh maybe sometime two mile, five mile," he replied. "I got dog called 'Lady.' She smart chow. She run on road like prize fighter, think it big sport. She start out sometime run two mile, get tired, stop and rest, them make bee-line home. One day Lady she pretty close run me dead. She get started, keep going, keep going. I run beat the devil keep up. I say Lady lop moki hop li chow suey, wook o son of fun shuey, you never stop. I run twenty mile and all time chow dog follow rabbit track and she not come back yet. No let chow dog train me no more."

GOOD FINISH FOR BAD MEN

SHOOTING ROBBERS CAPTURED OUTSIDE SAN BERNARDINO
LAST OF THE REAL DESPERADOES NOW GOING TO PRISON
ENCOUNTER WITH YIDDISH PEDDLER MARKS THE END

George Herriman would stay on at the *Los Angeles Times* from January through August, 1906. Before the winter was out he would be back on the Hearst payroll, working primarily as an editorial cartoonist for the *Los Angeles Herald Examiner,* but also experimenting regularly now with various new comic strip ideas — a process of experimentation which would lead seven years later to the world's first *Krazy Kat* daily comic strip on October 28, 1913.

Before he would leave the *Times,* however, Herriman would be sent back out to the field once more, this time to illustrate the closing of one of the old West's last frontiers — the capture, in fact, of the last two badmen to terrorize the old dirt trails and highways of early California. Jake and Silas Castile had been taken outside San Bernardino. As the Times reported, what with the capture of the two men most feared throughout the region for "the enjoyment" they seemed to take in stealing horses, shooting up border towns, and robbing people along the highway, "southern Californians could now climb out of their cyclone cellars, and breathe a sigh of relief."

Ironically, the Castile brothers seemed to owe their arrest to a certain Ikey Morris, a modest Russian-born Jewish tailor, who had been robbed and beaten by the brothers during the night, but who had escaped to inform the local authorities of the brothers' whereabouts by the next morning.

Playing their role to the hilt, the Castile Brothers remained unrepentant right to the last. After waking the next morning they made one final loot and pillage tour of the old neighborhood before they were spotted outside San Bernardino "wearing scowls so diabolical that even the local dogs are afraid to bark."

Just before they were captured, Silas Castile was identified by Ike Morris as the man actually driving the wagon, while his brother was observed sitting alongside him, flashing a pistol in the morning sun, and shooting at just about anything that moved.

Thanks to Ikey Morris, the Brothers were intercepted by a fairly large posse, brought to a trial rather quickly, and sentenced to spend the rest of their days behind the bars at San Quentin.

Herriman was there at this turning, just as he had been there for most of the major turnings of this decade. A new world was taking form here at the edge of the desert, and George Herriman, more than most, would help to create its new mythologies. And this new world would have its own new myths and heroes. The age of the Castile Brothers was passing; it would not be long before characters like Ikey Morris, the Jewish tailor; or the Little Tramp, Charlie Chaplin; or Leopold Bloom, the Dublin merchant; would begin to speak convincingly as the new century's Everyman, or just plain everyperson, as the century would eventually demand; and that a kat like Krazy — dear Mother Krazy — could become so damnably beautiful, "the tenderest monster of our new mythology," simply in her insistence that "the whole woild really is beautiful," but only if you have taken the time to turn everything on its tail.

A brand new American century was arriving on the streets of Los Angeles in 1906. Rendering that world as he uniquely imagined it, George Herriman was an important gatekeeper to the full, divine, comic range of the new American popular arts and culture which would come to pass. It was Spring, and it was Ragtime. All the foolish mices, and all the fey dear kats would most assuredly now learn how to swing.

BOB CALLAHAN was an award-winning poet, author and journalist. He edited The New Comics Anthology, The New Smithsonian Book of Comic Book Stories, *and* The Big Book of Irish-American Culture, *and co-founded, with Art Spiegelman, the short-lived Neon Lit graphic crime novel series whose releases included Paul Karasik and David Mazzucchelli's radical reinterpretation of Paul Auster's* City of Glass. *He also co-wrote the on-line comic strip* Dark Hotel. *Callahan died in 2008.*

1919.

Readers, please note: an Ignatz "dingbat" placed
below a strip indicates a relevant or related footnote
at the volume's end for that particular selection,
all to be found in the "Ignatz Debaffler" section.

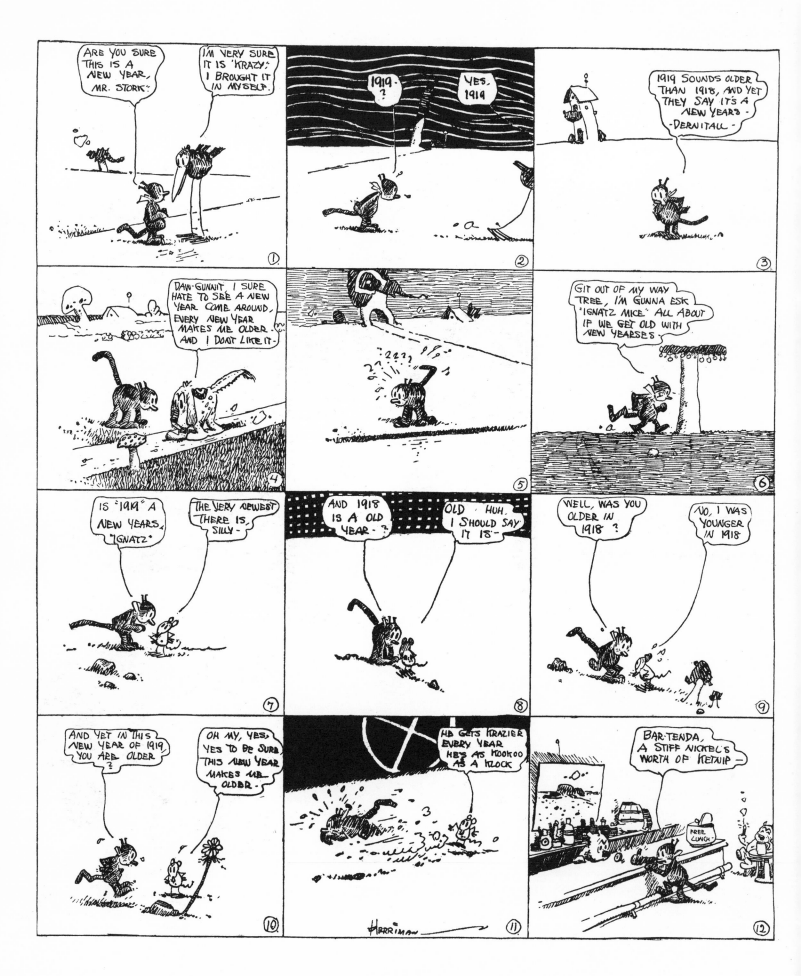

January 5th, 1919.

January 12th, 1919.

January 19th, 1919.

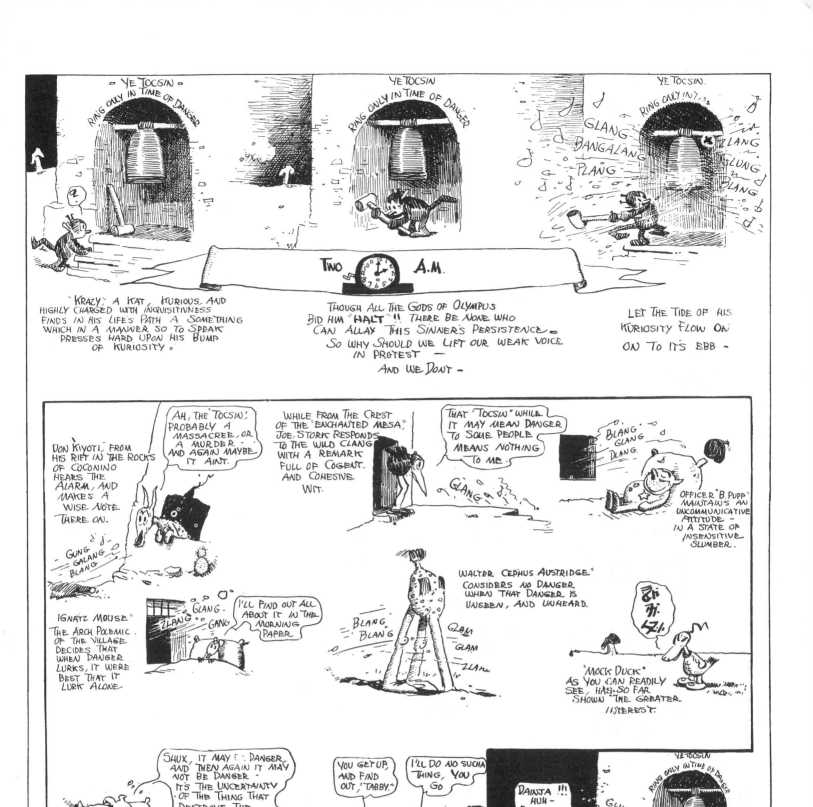

January 26th, 1919.

19.

February 2nd, 1919.

February 9th, 1919.

February 16th, 1919.

February 23rd, 1919.

March 2nd, 1919.

March 9th, 1919.

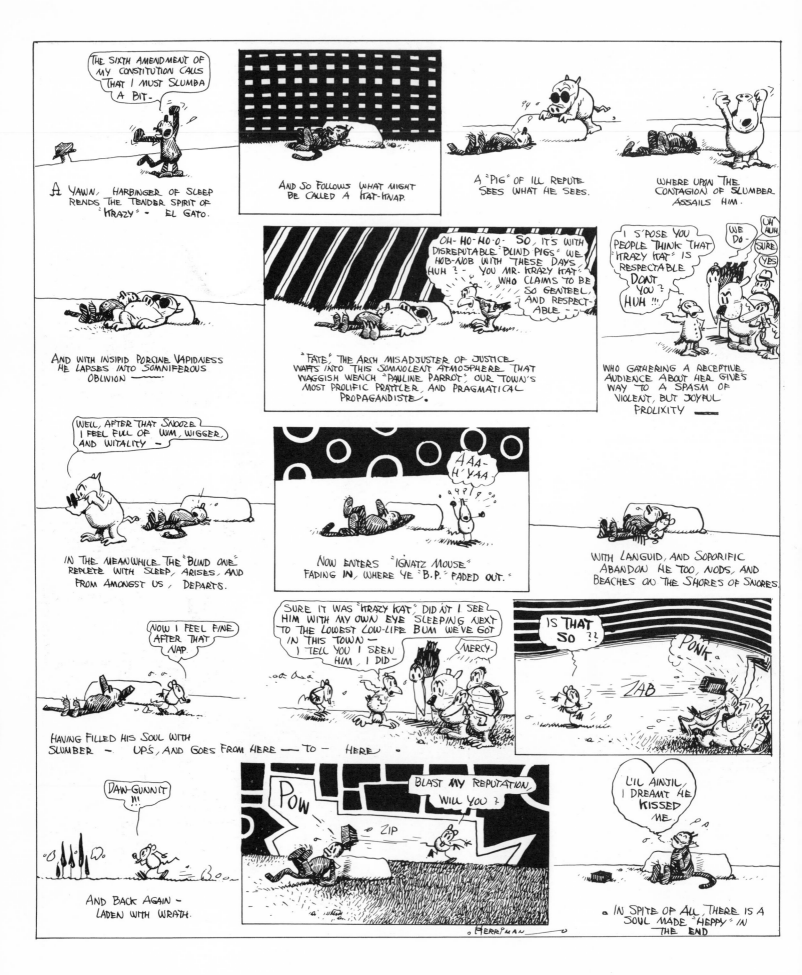

March 16th 1919.

March 23rd, 1919.

March 30th, 1919.

April 6th, 1919.

April 13th, 1919.

April 20th, 1919.

April 27th, 1919.

May 4th, 1919.

May 11th, 1919.

May 18th, 1919.

May 25th, 1919.

June 1st, 1919.

June 8th, 1919.

June 15th, 1919.

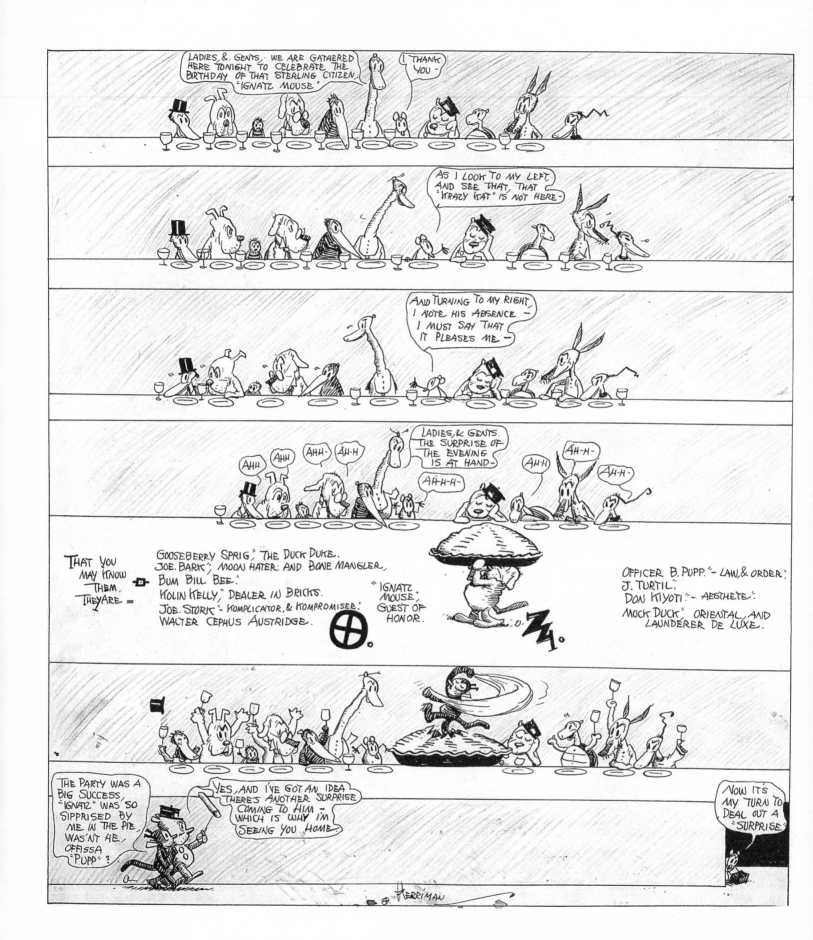

June 22nd, 1919.

June 29th, 1919.

July 6th, 1919.

July 13th, 1919.

July 20th, 1919.

July 27th, 1919.

August 3rd, 1919.

August 10th, 1919.

August 17th, 1919.

August 24th, 1919.

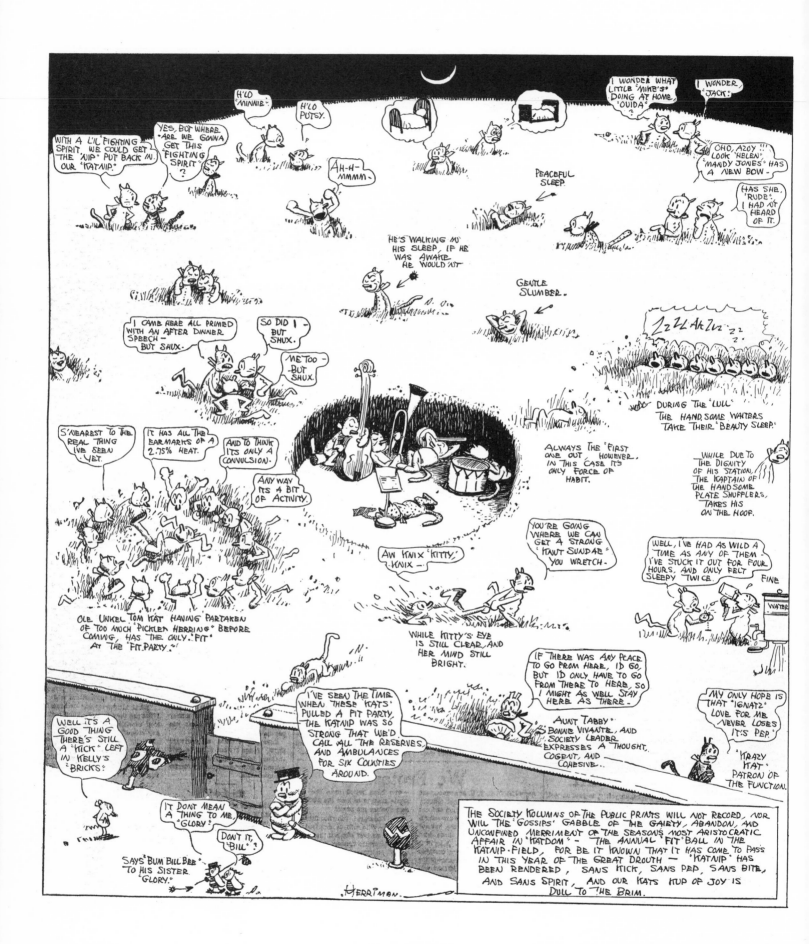

August 31st, 1919.

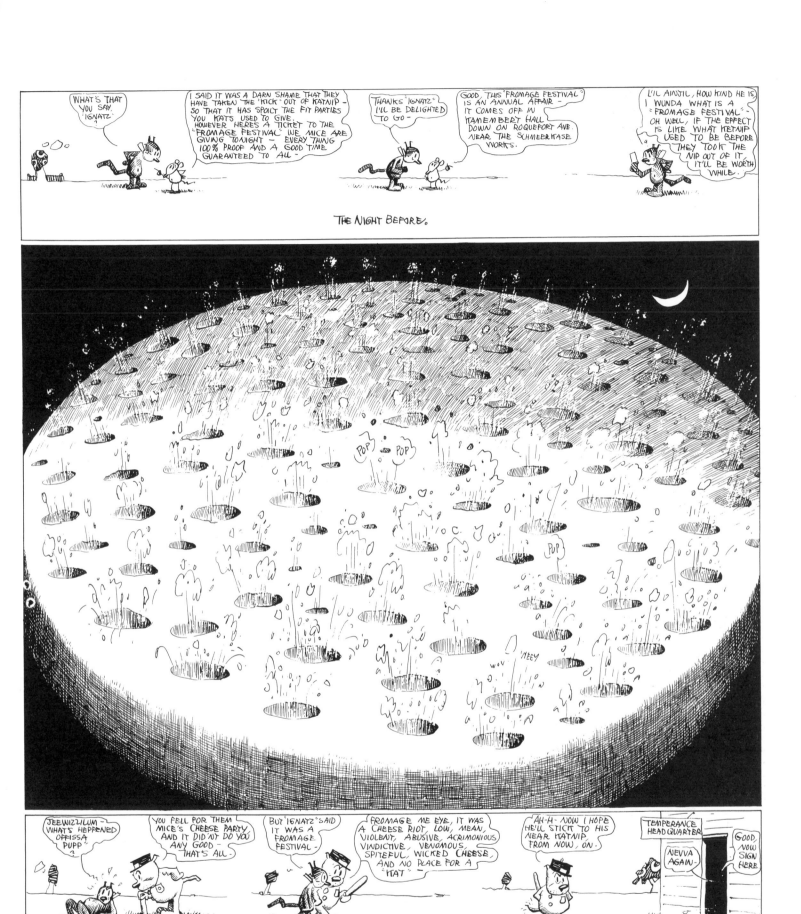

The Night Before.

The Morning After.

September 7th, 1919.

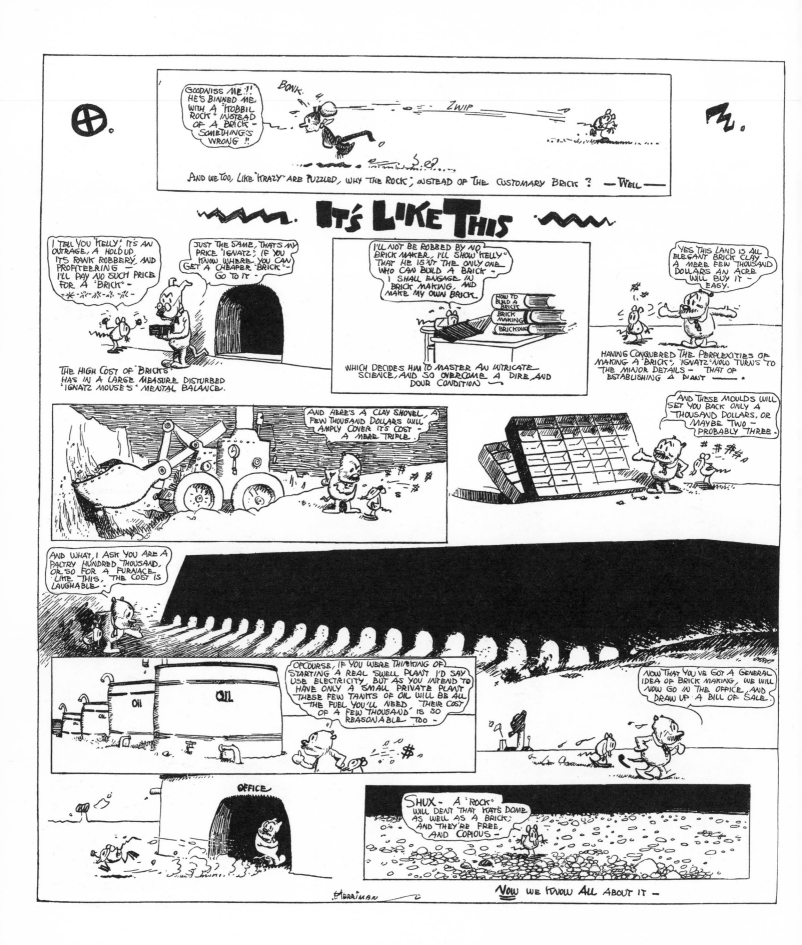

September 14th, 1919.

September 21st, 1919.

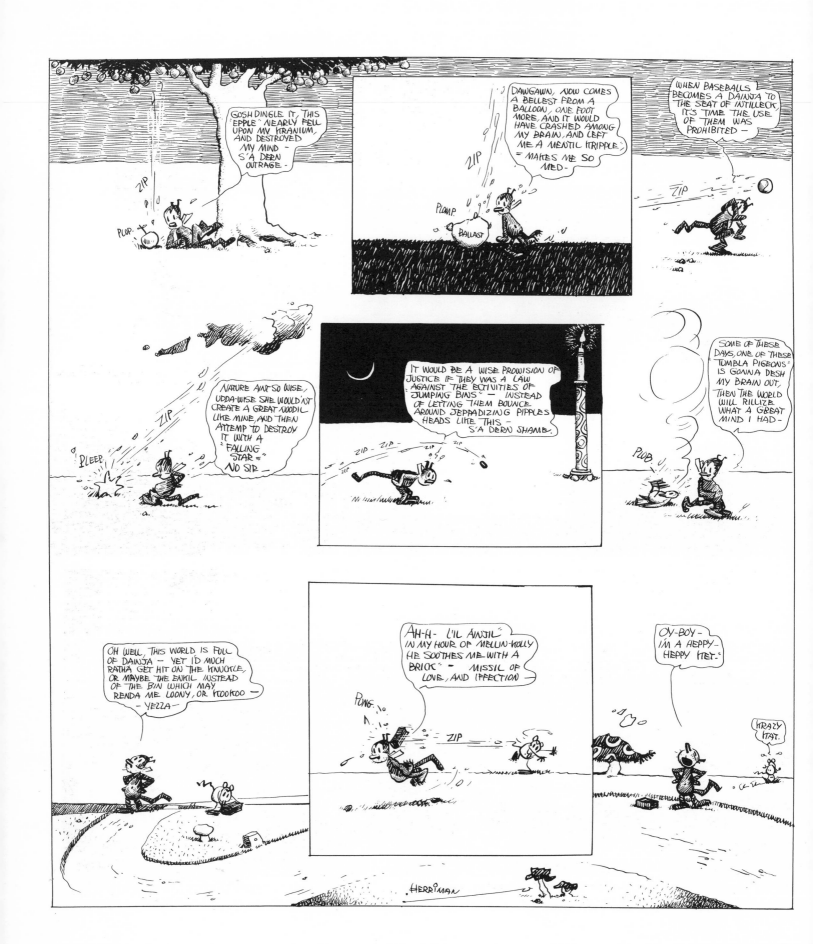

September 28th, 1919.

October 5th, 1919.

October 12th, 1919.

October 19th, 1919.

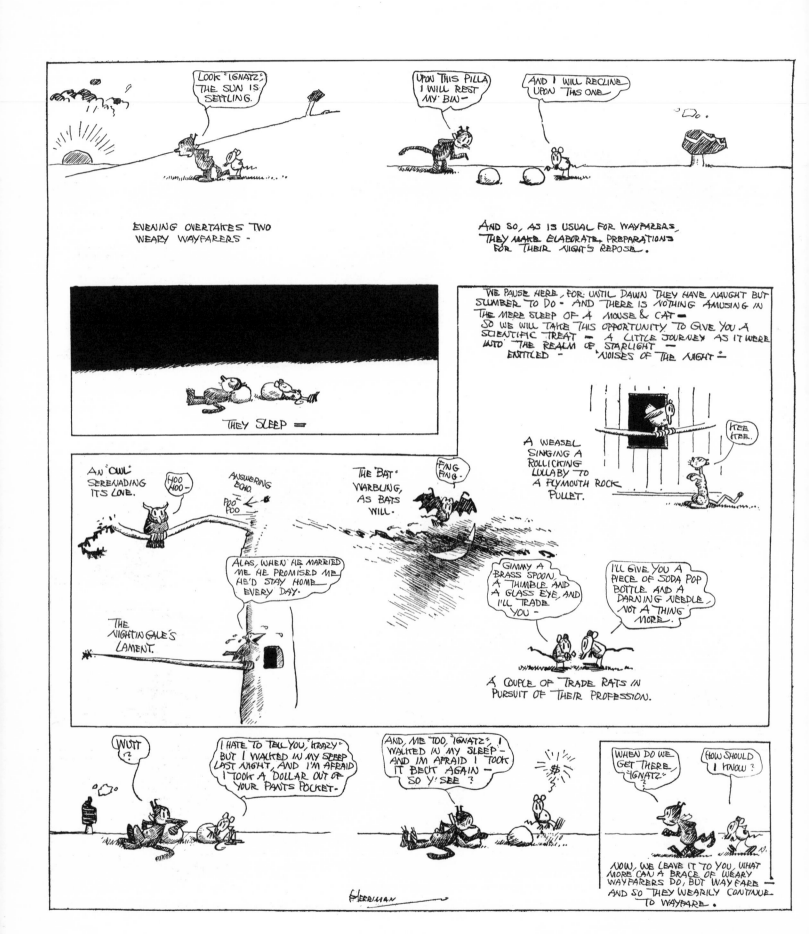

October 26th, 1919.

November 2nd, 1919.

November 9th, 1919.

"WINTER !!!"

BEHOLD HIM, "IGNATZ MOUSE," · LIKE ALL HIS TRIBE, DEPILATED, FURLESS, AND BALD, WHILE ALL ELSE IN THE WORLD BUT THE FROG, AND THE ANGLE WORM ARE HIRSUTE AND CLOTHED IN FUR · BUT, HARK TO A TALE OF BETTER DAYS, WHEN —— MICE HAD FUR —— YES, FUR –

LONG, LONG AGO; AT A PERIOD OF TIME VERY DISTANT FROM NOW, IN THAT GOLDEN PRE-RATRAP, AND PRE-CASEOUS AGE, MICE SCAMPERED ABOUT CLOTHED IN FUR, FUR SILKEN IN SHEEN, AND TEXTURE, LONG OF LENGTH, AND OF SUCH WARMTH AS TO REBUFF WITH IMPUNITY THE FURY OF ALL THE HOSTS OF WINTER —

ONE NIGHT THE SUN PASSED OUT, AND WITH NO GREATER CEREMONY THAN EASING IT SELF OVER THE WESTERN HORIZON, LEFT THE MOUSE WORLD FLAT, TO DARKNESS, AND ASTONISHMENT.

THEN CAME TO THEM "AMBROSE MC KNIBBIL", BEARING A "CANDLE," BROUGHT FROM A DISTANT LAND, AND PEOPLE, THE FIRST OF ITS KIND UPON WHICH THE ACUTE EYE OF A "MOUSE" HAD EVER BEEN LAID —

AND ALL THROUGH THAT NIGHT, A NIGHT MADE DAY WITH CANDLE LIGHT, MERRY MICE BASKED IN THE GLOW OF THEIR MAGIC TAPER · BUT ·

EVEN IN THAT EARLY DAY, AS THE CANDLE CANNOT GO TO THE "MOTH," THE "MOTH" MUST COME TO THE CANDLE, AND HE CAME, IN MULTITUDES HE CAME —

AND AS "MOTHS" WILL, LINGERED UNTIL THE LAST FLUTTER OF CANDLE LIGHT FLICKERED INTO DARKNESS IN ITS POOL OF TALLOW.

THE SUN, MORE FAITHFUL, MORE LASTING THAN A TAPER OF TALLOW, RISES UPON A SCENE OF DESOLATION FOR THE "MOTHS," WHEN THE CANDLE LIGHT HAD CEASED HAD FOUND A FERTILE FIELD OF MOUSE FUR TO FEED UPON, AND HAVING FED, FLOWN LEAVING TO POSTERITY A MOUSE PEOPLE,

I WISH NATURE WOULD DISCONTINUE HAVING WINTA, OR ELSE GIVE "IGNATZ" A COAT OF FUR – IT AINT FAIR

.HERRIMAN

BARE, BALD, AND NUDE SOME SAY ITS NATURE'S WORK, BUT WE KNOW BETTER, IT WAS "MOTHS."

November 16th, 1919.

November 23rd, 1919.

November 30th, 1919.

SHIPS THAT PASS IN THE NIGHT, WHENCE DO THEY COME, AND WHITHER DO THEY GO?
AND SO "KURIOSITY" IS BORN IN THE PALPITATING BOSOM OF "KRAZY KAT" "KURIOSITY" UNREQUITED,
AND UNSATISFIED AS THE OBJECTS OF HIS INQUISITIVENESS LIE IN AN ELEMENT FORBIDDEN TO KATS –
QUANTITIES OF OCEAN, MULTITUDES OF WATER.

December 7th, 1919.

December 14th, 1919.

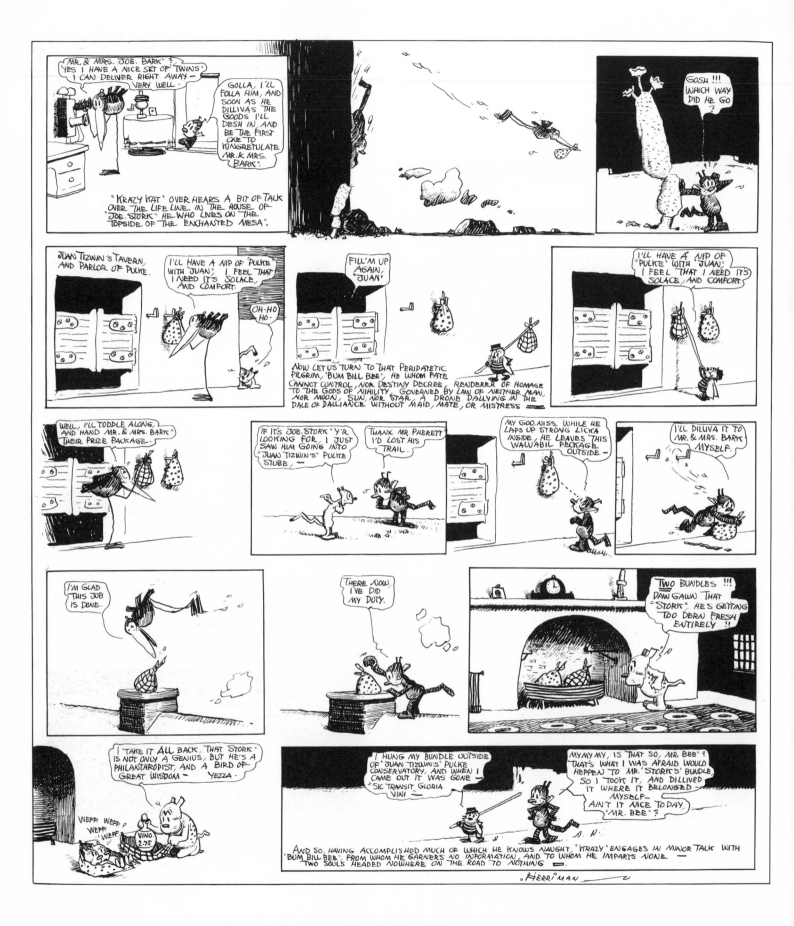

December 21st, 1919.

MANY THINGS HAVE STALKED THROUGH "COCONINO", AND YET HAVE LEFT BUT LITTLE IMPRESS UPON THAT ASTUTE DEMOCRATIC COMMUNITY —
BUT YESTERDAY, "ROYALTY" IN THE SHAPE OF A "KING" STRUTTED INTO THEIR MIDST, AND EVERY SOUL AMONG
THEM WAS SHAKEN TO ITS VERY CENTER —

"KRISTOPHER KACKIL", ONCE LEADER OF THE POPULIST TICKET, LETS IT BE KNOWN THAT HE IS NOW IN THE KING'S GOOD GRACES, HAVING BEEN MADE LORD HIGH BREAKFAST ANNOUNCER, AND IMPERIAL KAPON TO THE KOURT —

"MOCK DUCK" NO LONGER DEALS WITH THE PROLETARIAT, BEING NOW THE ROYAL LAUNDERER, AND SHIRT MANGLER TO HIS MAJESTY —

"KOLIN KELLY" DEALER IN BRICKS NO LONGER ATTIRES HIMSELF IN THE EMBLEM OF TRUE REPUBLICANISM THE "BINOCLE", SINCE HIS ATTACHMENT TO THE KING'S PERSON AS CUSTODIAN OF THE IMPERIAL BRICK, HE NOW BASKS IN THE SHEEN OF ROYALTY WITH HIS EYE DECKED OUT IN A SET OF ONE CYLINDER CHEATERS, THE "MONOCLE".

WALTER CEPHUS AUSTRIDGE, THE KALAHARAN DICKY-BIRD, WHOSE WEARING OF A CELULOID DICKY HAS LONG PROCLAIMED HIS STAUNCH DEMOCRATIC SPIRIT HAS FALLEN PRONE FOR MONARCHICAL BLANDISHMENTS, AND IS NOW CHIEF PROVIDER OF PLUMES TO THE QUEEN, FOR WHICH HE HAS BEEN DUBBED "KNIGHT OF THE FEATHER".

MENIAL, AND REPUBLICAN FAMILIES WILL WAIT IN VAIN FOR THE THRILL WHICH ATTENDS THE PERIODICAL VISITS OF "JOE. STORK" THAT MOST DEMOCRATIC OF BIRDS — BE IT KNOWN THAT HE IS NOW ALLIED TO THE ROYAL HOUSEHOLD AS SPECIAL PURVEYOR OF PRINCESSES, PRINCES, AND QUINCES TO THEIR MAJESTIES —

IGNATZ MOUSE IS NOW LORD HIGH CHAMBERLAIN OF THE ROYAL CHEESE.

"OFFICER B. PUPP" IS NO MORE A PUBLIC SERVANT, ENFORCING LAW, AND ORDER, BUT CONSTABLE IN THE KING'S GUARDS.

AND SO IT ALL WENT, UNTIL "KRAZY" THE KAT, WHO HAD TAKEN ADVANTAGE OF THAT GREAT BOON ACCORDED TO KATS, AND HAD LOOKED A LONG WEARY EYE FULL UPON THE KING ———— (CONTINUED PICTORIALLY BELOW.).

WHILE DEMOCRACY TOTTERED ON THE BRINK, AND KINGHOOD THREATENED THE EQUIPOISE OF LIBERTY, "KRAZY KAT" IN HIS OWN SIMPLE WAY SHOWS HIS FELLOW "COCONINOANS" THAT A KAT MAY NOT ONLY LOOK "AT" A KING, BUT WITH THE USE OF HIS LONG TAIL, TOMATO-CAN, UMBRELLA, AND THE AID OF A KOUPLE OF KRAZY KITTENS HE CAN LOOK "LIKE" A KING — A LESSON WHICH CERTAIN PROSELYTES TO ROYALTY (NOT ENTIRELY BEREFT OF INTELLIGENCE) TOOK WELL TO MIND, AND HEART ————.

THAT VERY NIGHT, "ROYALTY" RODE OUT OF "COCONINO", BY RAIL — AIDED BY IT'S LOYAL, IF NOT ROYAL SUPPORTERS ———.

—HERRIMAN—

December 28th, 1919.

———

1920.

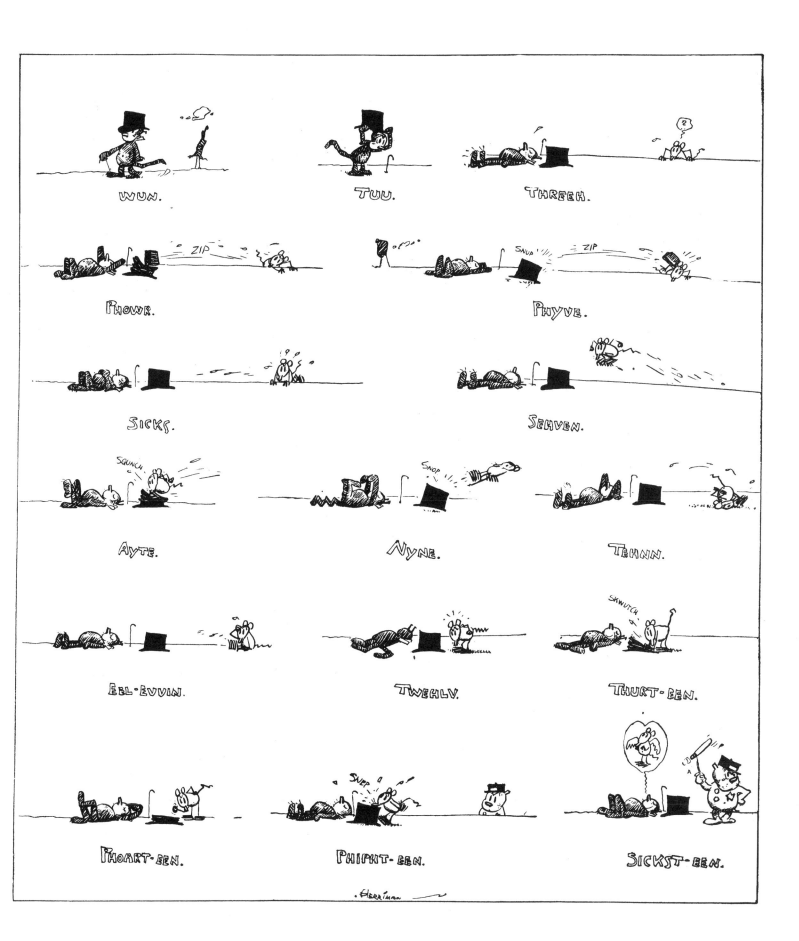

January 4th, 1920.

January 11th, 1920.

January 18th, 1920.

January 25th, 1920.

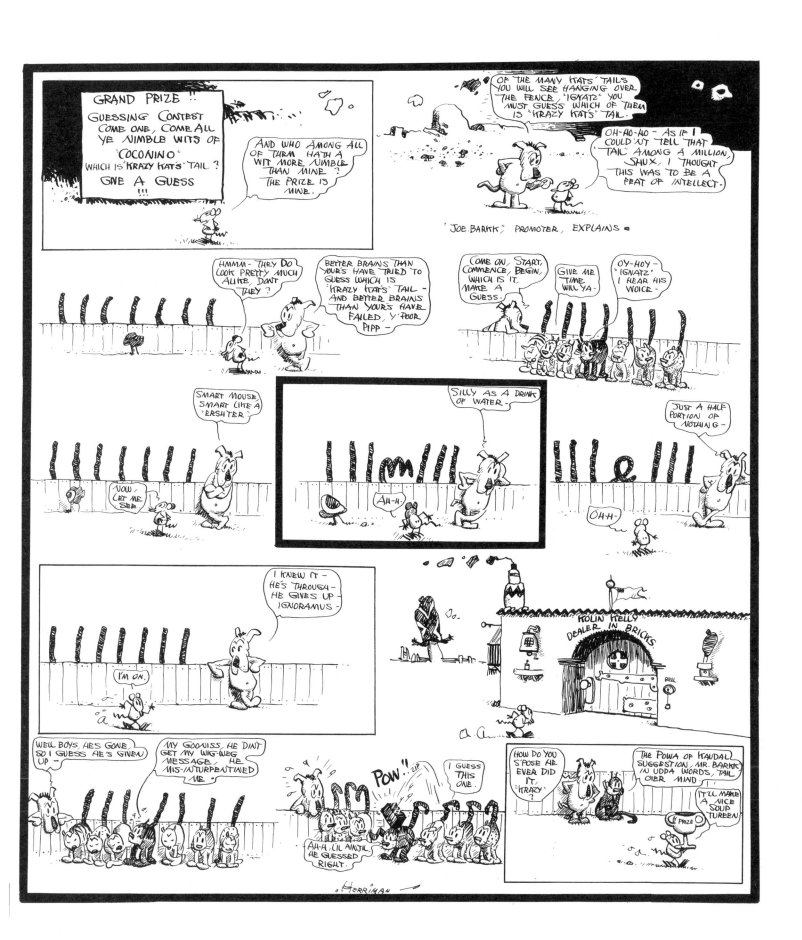

February 1st, 1920.

February 8th, 1920.

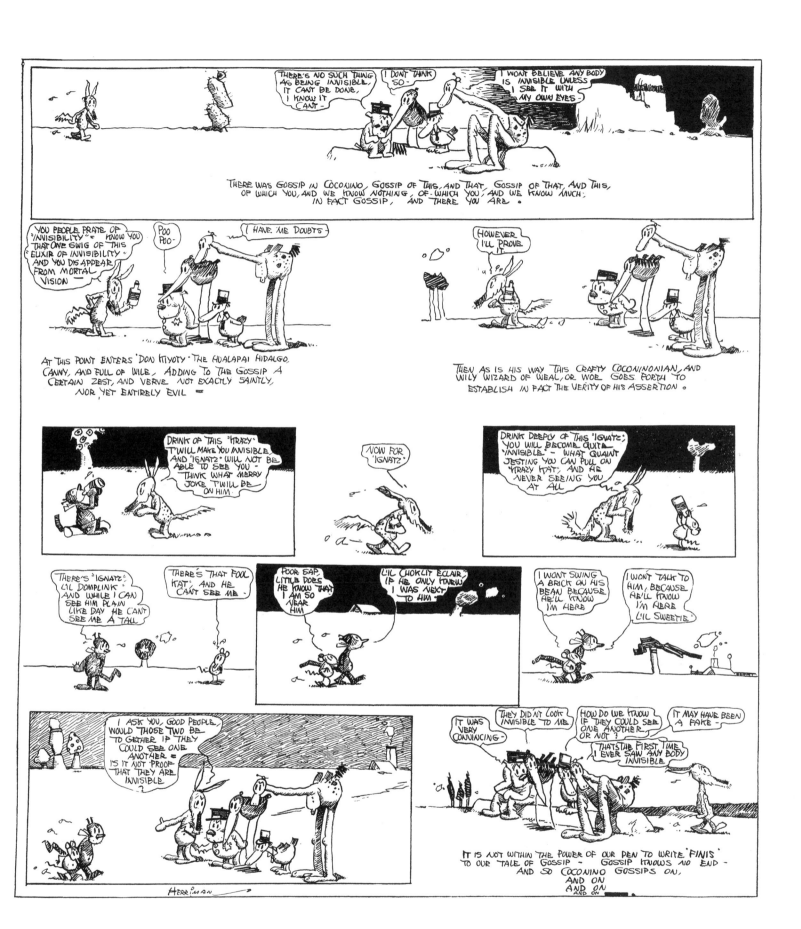

February 22nd, 1920.

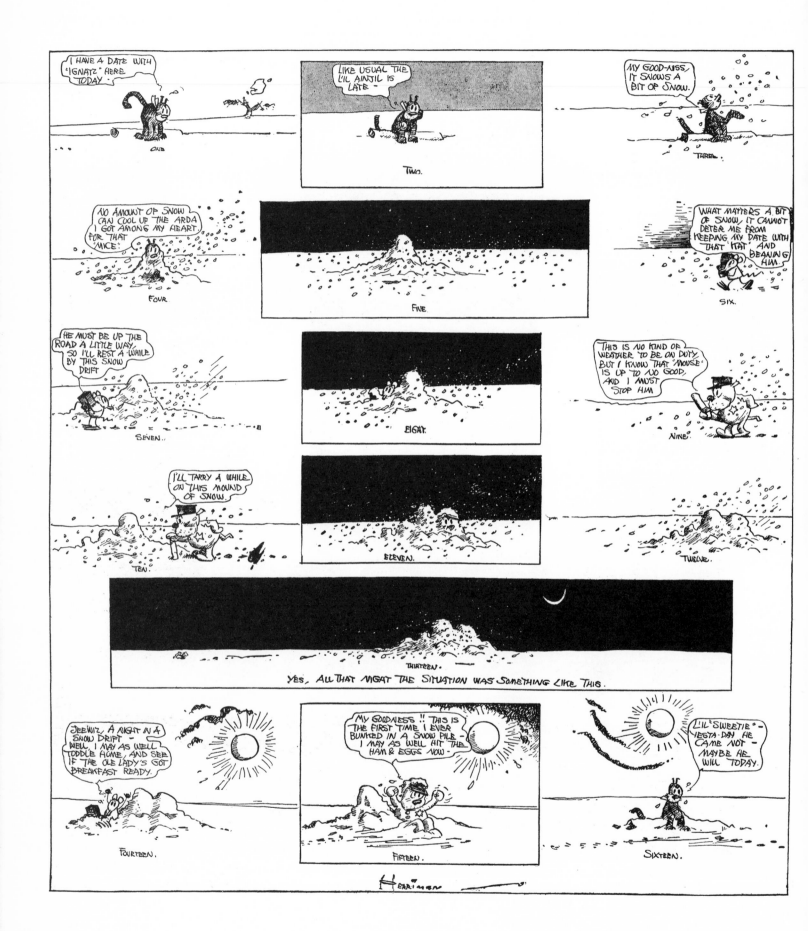

February 29th, 1920.

March 7th, 1920.

March 14th, 1920.

March 21st, 1920.

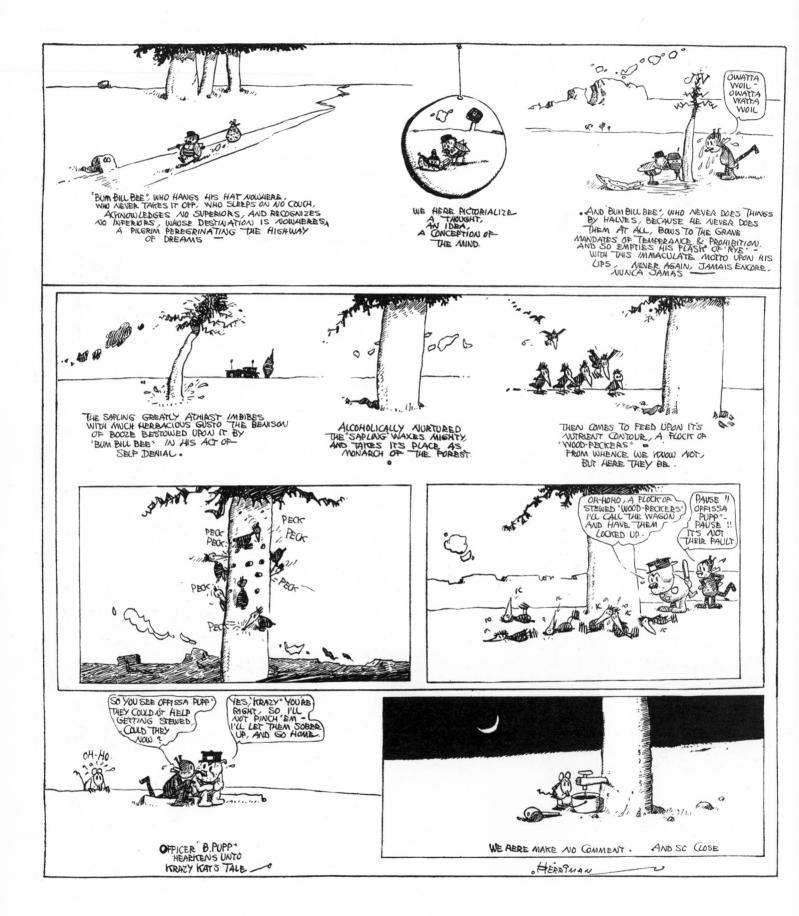

March 28th, 1920.

April 4th, 1920.

THERE BE THOSE
BRISTLING OF BRAIN,
DEEP OF MIND, AND
OF GREAT GIRTH OF CRANIUM,

BUT
SHORT OF SENTIMENT,
NARROW OF HEART,
AND PYGMIES OF PASSION,
WHO TELL US IN
WIDE, AND WIELDY WORDS
WEIGHTY WITH WISDOM
THAT THE 'MOON'
IS COLD —

SO MUCH FOR
THEM

NOW 'TO THOSE OF YOU WHO HAVE NOT LATELY
LOOKED UPON 'LUNA'S' LILY FACE WE BEG THAT YOU DO
SO AT THIS MOMENT FOR SHE WILL IN GREAT
MEASURE BE AN IMPORTANT MEMBER IN THE
ARGUMENT WE ARE ABOUT TO
DEAL TO YOU

SHE CAME TO ME A MAIDEN 'OSTRICH', OVER THE
SANDS OF THE 'KALAHARI', AND WITH HER COMING
ROSE THE MOON, FULL AND RESPLENDENT, AND SO
WITH MOON IN MY HEART I ASKED HER TO BE MINE,
WITH MOON IN HER SOFT BLUE EYE SHE ANSWERED YES,
WITH MOON IN OUR SOULS WE WERE WED,
SOON CAME 'JUNE', CAME A HANDSOME BUCKO
OF AN 'EMU', AND WITH
MOON IN THEIR HEARTS
THEY LEFT ME FLAT —
— 'TWAS MOON THAT
WARMED MY BEING,
AND 'TWAS MOON
THAT CHILLED IT —
AND THAT'S ALL I
GOTTA SAY ABOUT
MOONS

WALTER CEPAUS AUSTRIDGE, A BIRD IN WHOSE BRAIN IS
SEATED A GREAT SENSE OF SCIENCE, AND IN WHOSE
HEART FLARES THE FIRES OF ROMANCE, AND BY WHOSE
GREAT LENGTH OF NECK THESE TWO EMOTIONS ARE KEPT
IN FRIENDLY, AND UNCLASHING DISTANCE, ALL OF
WHICH QUALIFIES HIM TO GIVE A DUAL OPINION OF
THE SUBJECT WITH WHICH WE DEAL, AND WHICH HE
GIVES WITH MAGNIFICENT AUSTRIDGIAN CLARITY.

THROUGH MANY 'CANICULAR' DAYS I HAVE GONE WITHOUT BEING
MOVED TO SO MUCH AS A WHIMPER, I HAVE GAZED WITH A
COOL UNRUFFLED EYE UPON COMETS, STARS, PLANETS,
ASTEROIDS, RAINBOWS, AURORA-BOREALISES, AND SUNS
WITH CANINE EQUANIMITY, YET LET MY VISION REST
BUT A MOMENT UPON EVEN A MERE FRAGMENT OF
MOON' THEN IS MY WHOLE BEING MOVED TO SONG
TO BARK, TO YODLE, I MUST LIFT MY VOICE IN CAROL
IN LILT, AND LULLABY, IN YELP, AND HOWL —
I'M NO MOON EXPERT, BUT I'LL SAY AS HOW
A 'MOON' HAS STRANGE
POWERS OVER A
HOUND'S VOCAL
LAYOUT

JOE. BARKK; EMINENT BONE CRUSHER, AND
TAIL WAGGER GIVES A FEW ELUCIDATIVE
VOCABLES TOUCHING ON, AND APPERTAINING TO
'MOONS' — MOONS AS IS, AND
MOONS AS AIN'T
YET WITH HALF AN EYE WE CAN
PLAINLY SEE IT'S MOONS
HE MEANS.

I AM AT BEST BUT A TRIFLING TROUBADOUR, A
MEAGER MINSTREL WITH NO GREAT GIFT OF
MELODY, YET, IF BUT A RAY OF 'MOON'
BENDS IT'S WAY OVER THE DESERT'S EDGE,
MY VOICE WILL BURST INTO WILD CADENCE,
AND SEND BACK FROM EVERY ROCK A THOUSAND
ECHOES, AND EVERY EAR UPON WHICH THE
THRILL, AND TRILL OF MY MOON MAD VESPERS
FALL WILL SWEAR THAT THERE BE A
MILLION OF ME IN SONG — OUTSIDE OF
THAT I DON'T KNOW A DERN THING
ABOUT MOONS.

DON KIYOTI, SUAVE ANDALUSIAN HIDALGO, SUBTLE,
AND FILLED WITH WILE, WHO RANGES THE REACHES
OF NIGHT SOFTLY AS A CLOUD IN TRANSIT,
GENTLY AS A ZEPHYR HOMING WESTWARD,
QUIETLY AS A FEATHER'S FALL, GIVES TO AN
INDIFFERENT WORLD A FEW WISE
HOBANIAN CRACKS CONCERNING 'MOONS'.

HOOT
MOON —

'MOONS TO 'OLIVER OWL' ARE
MOONS, JUST MOONS,
THAT'S ALL

MR. B. WOFFIL BATT
SHOWS NO INTEREST
WHATEVER IN MOONS:

MOONS IS MY FRIENDS — GOSH,
WHAT WOULD BECOME OF MY BUSINESS
IF THERE WAS NO PARK BENCHES,
RIVERS EDGES, SEA-SHORES, AND
MOONS DAW-GUNNIT,
ESPECIALLY MOONS.

'JOE. STORK', WHEN SEEN APERCH THE TOPSIDE
OF THE 'ENCHANTED MESA', HIS HOME —
ADMITTED THE GREAT VALUE OF 'MOONS'
IN CERTAIN CIRCLES.

OH-H- NIGHT OF LOVE,
OH-H-A NIGHT OF JUNE,
AND MOON —

THANK GOODNESS
THE MOON IS
SHINING, AND I
CAN SEE HIM
PLAINLY —

AH-H-H, LIL
MOON-BIMS

OTHERWISE I MIGHT
HAVE MISSED HIM,
AND WASTED A
PERFECTLY GOOD
'BRICK'

ZIP

OWATTA WOIL
WATTA WOIL
'MOON'
THIS WOULD BE
WITHOUT YOU —

WELL, WE STARTED OUT TO
ARGUE ABOUT THE 'MOON'S'
TEMPERATURE, AND AS USUAL
WE'VE RAMBLED QUITE A BIT,
AND IN THE END WE CAN ONLY
AGREE WITH 'KRAZY' — COLD, OR
WARM THE OLD 'MOON' SURE
HAS ITS USES —
AND THAT'S A FACT.

HERRIMAN

April 18th, 1920.

April 25th, 1920.

May 2nd, 1920.

May 9th, 1920.

May 16th, 1920.

May 23rd, 1920.

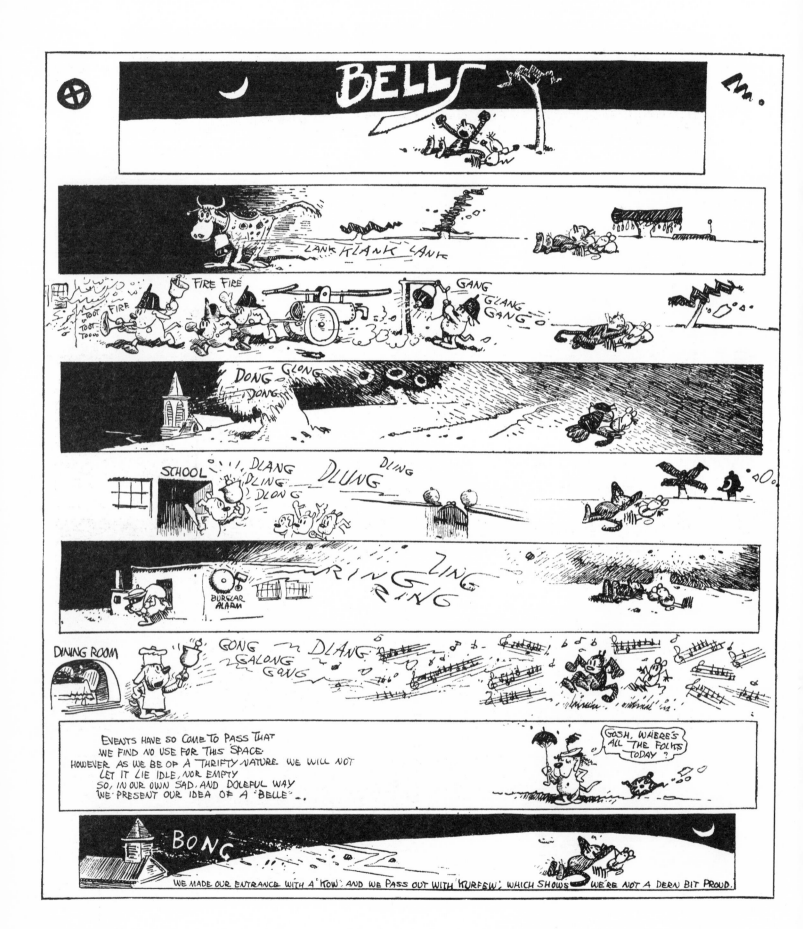

May 30th, 1920.

June 6th, 1920.

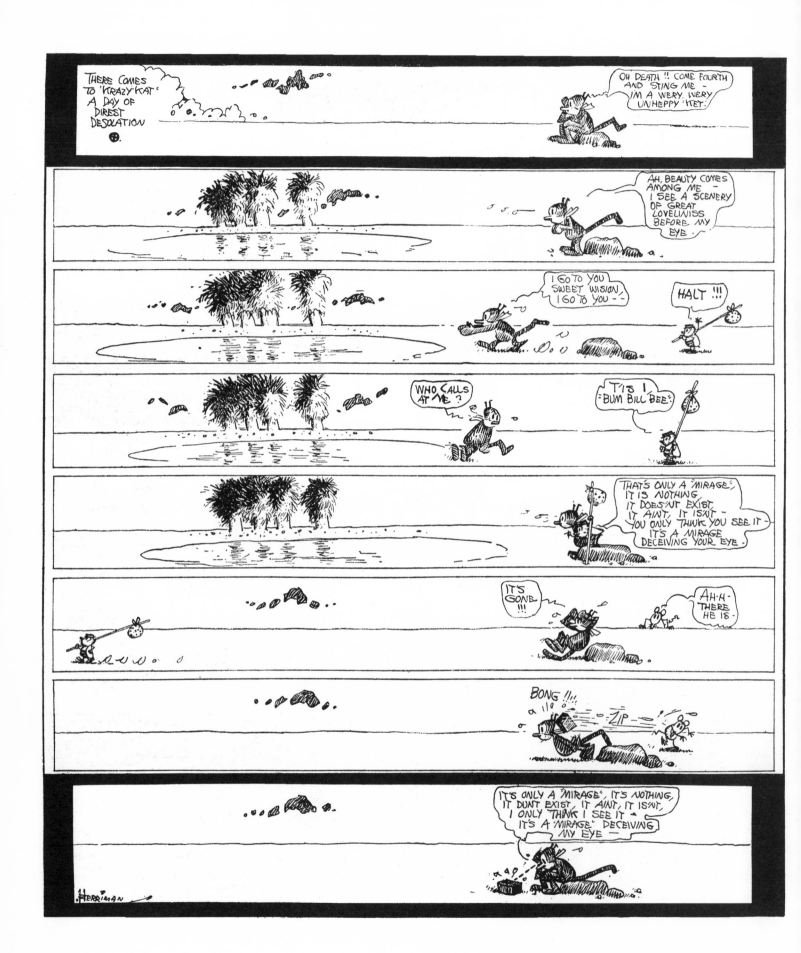

June 13th, 1920.

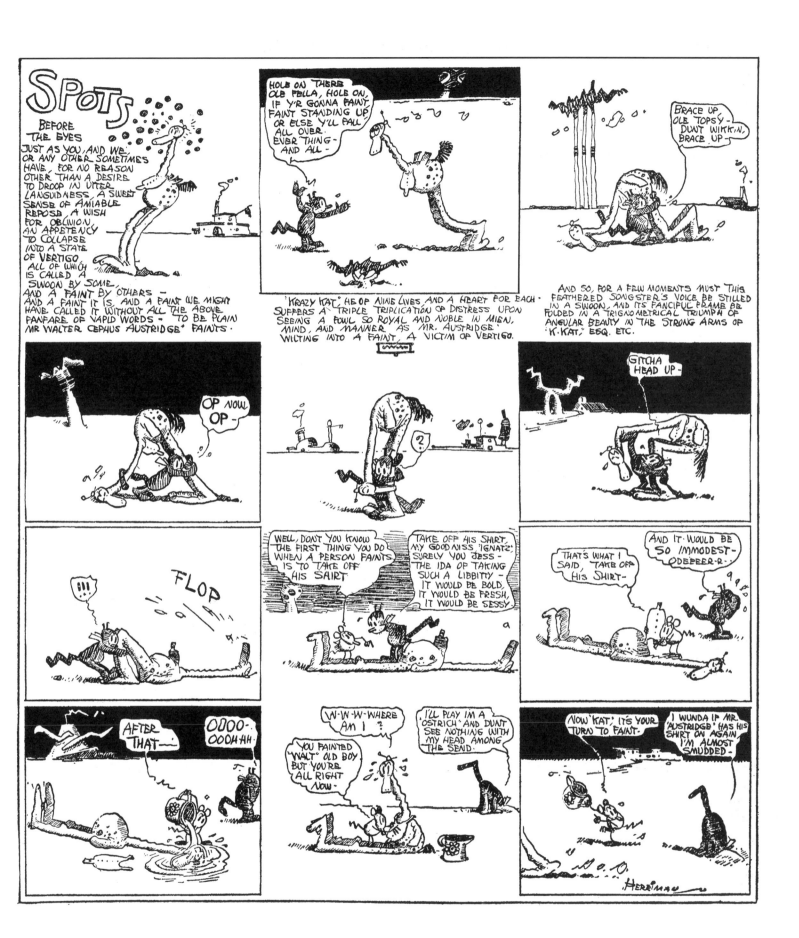

June 20th, 1920.

June 27th, 1920.

July 4th, 1920.

July 11th, 1920.

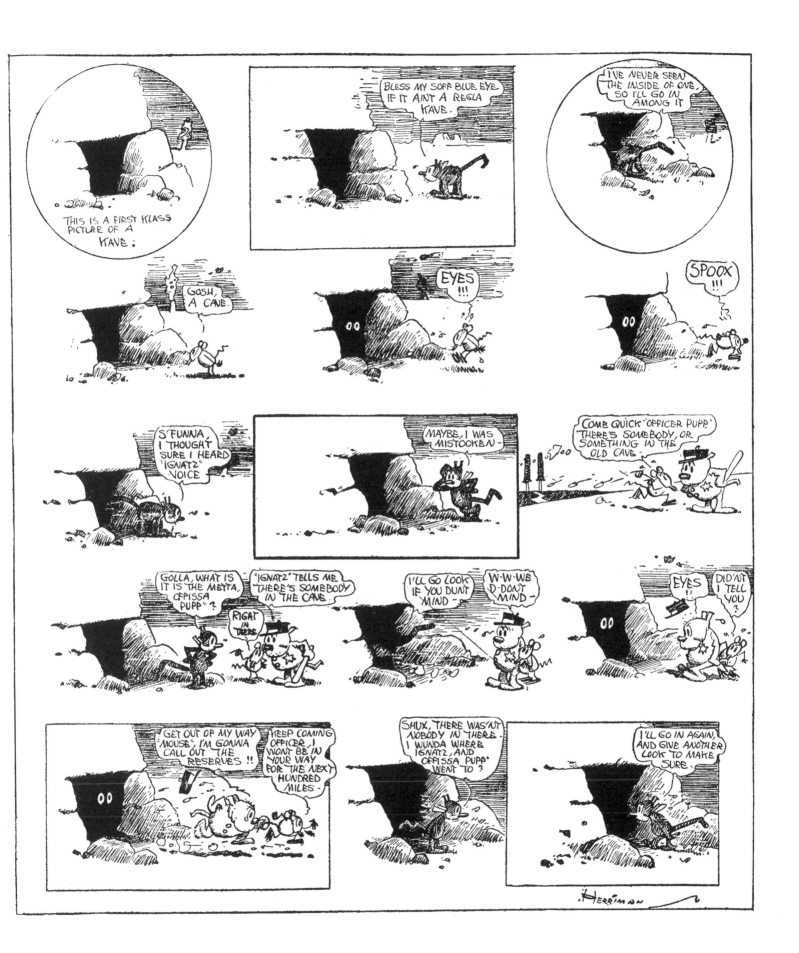

July 18th, 1920.

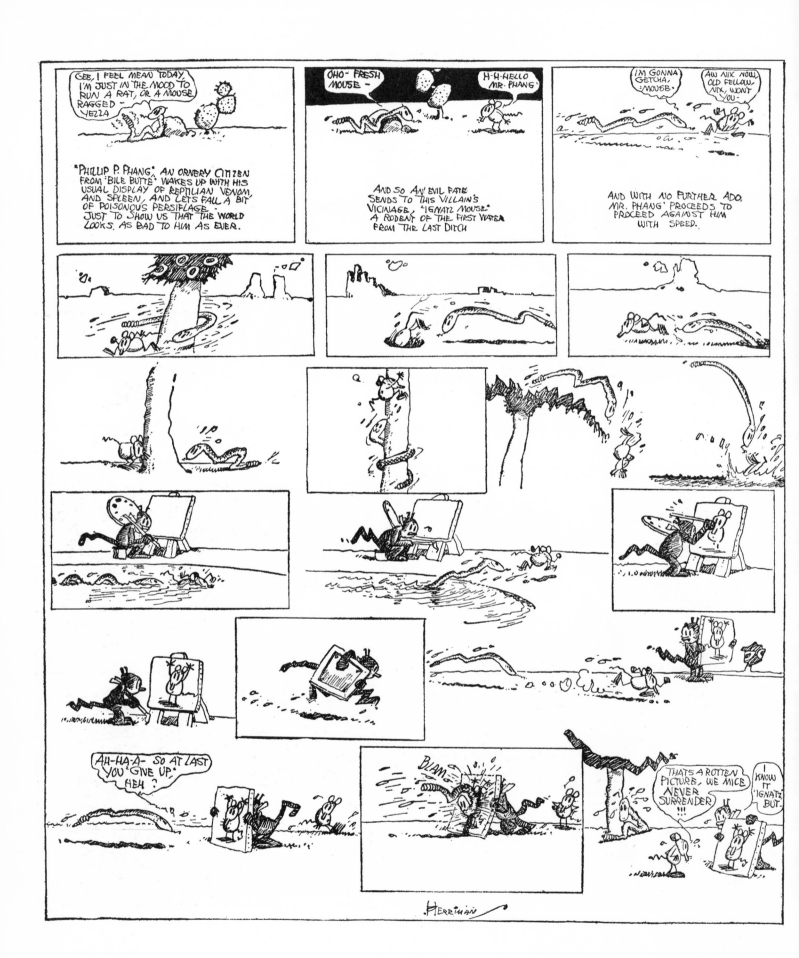

July 25th, 1920.

August 1st, 1920.

August 8th, 1920.

August 15th, 1920.

99.

August 22nd, 1920.

August 29th, 1920.

September 5th, 1920.

September 12th, 1920.

September 19th, 1920.

September 26th, 1920.

October 3rd, 1920.

October 10th, 1920.

October 17th, 1920.

October 24th, 1920.

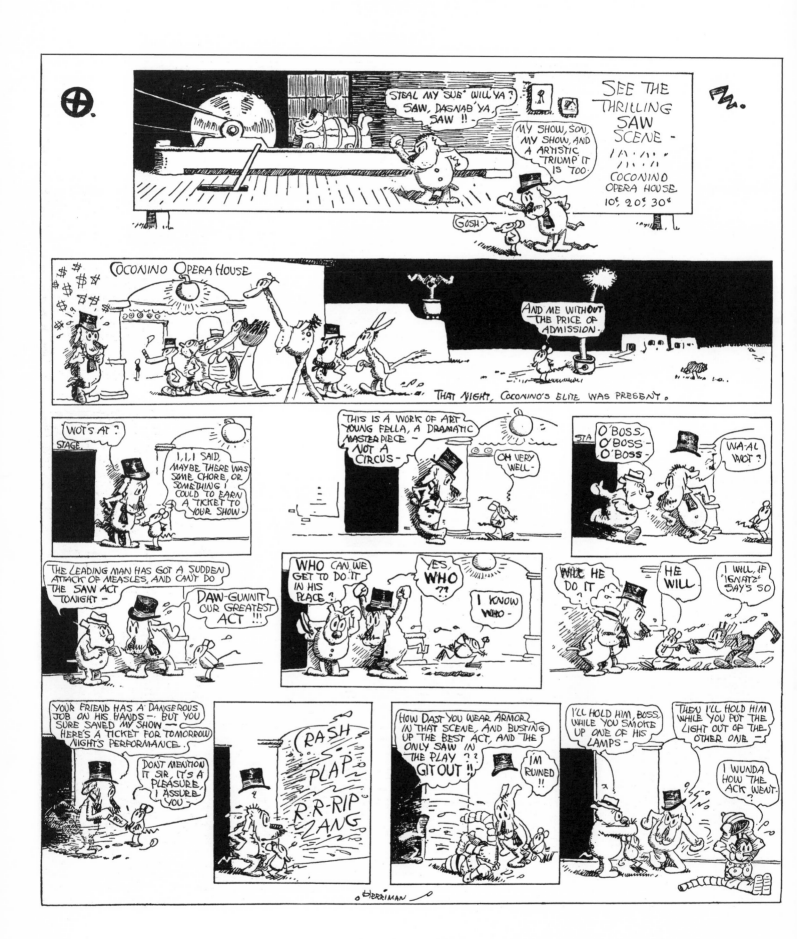

October 31st, 1920.

November 7th, 1920.

November 14th, 1920.

November 21st, 1920.

November 28th, 1920.

December 5th, 1920.

December 12th, 1920.

December 19th, 1920.

December 26th, 1920.

1921.

January 2nd, 1921.

January 9th, 1921.

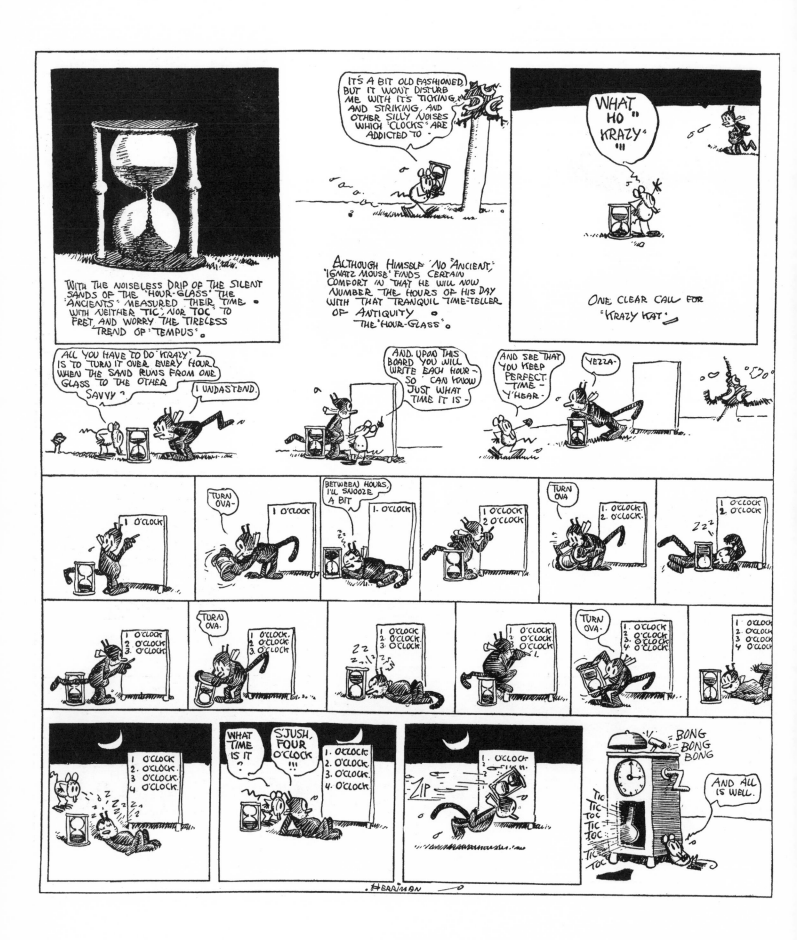

January 23rd, 1921.

January 30th, 1921.

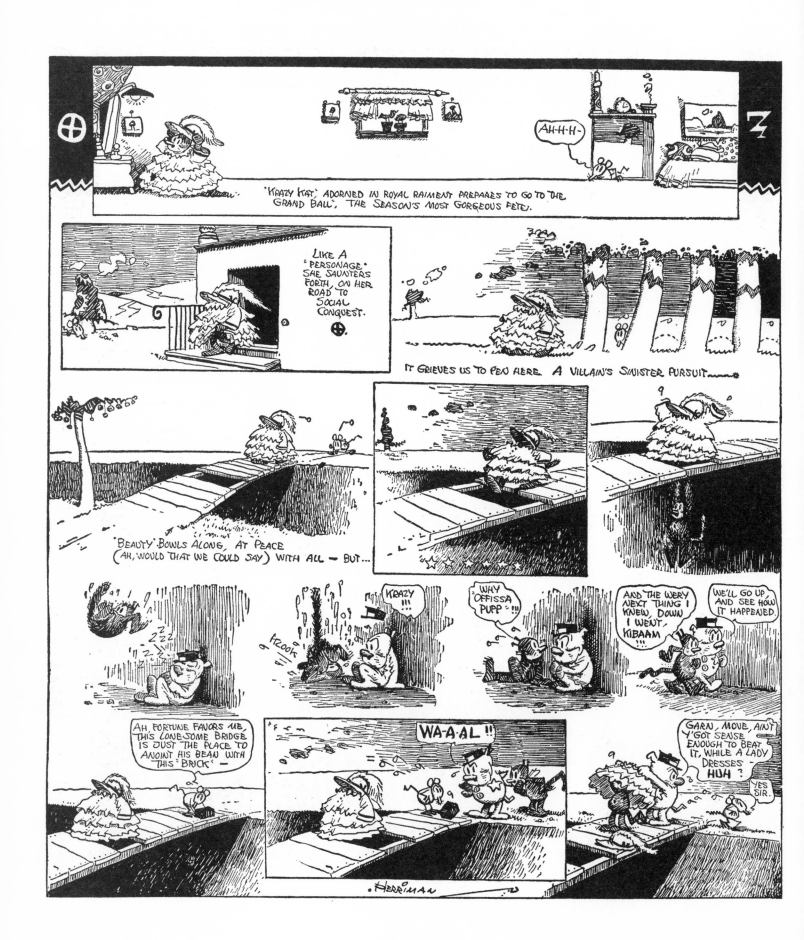

February 6th, 1921.

February 13th, 1921.

February 20th, 1921.

February 27th, 1921.

March 6th, 1921.

March 13th, 1921.

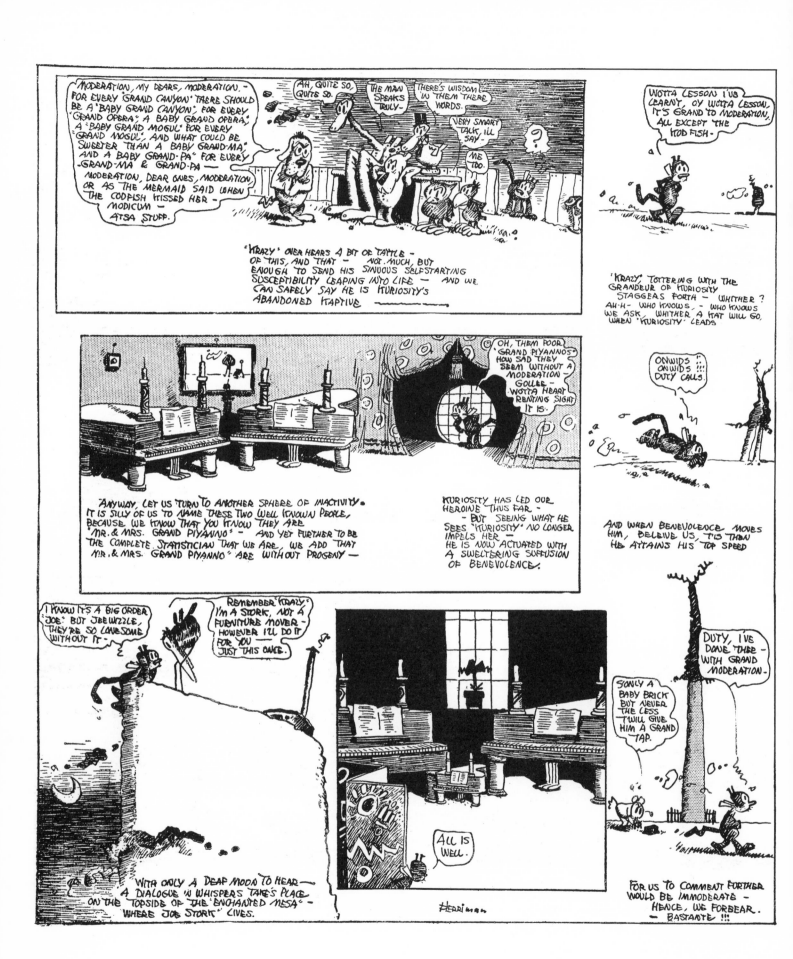

March 20th, 1921.

March 27th, 1921.

April 3rd, 1921.

April 10th, 1921.

April 17th, 1921.

April 24th, 1921.

May 1st, 1921.

May 8th, 1921.

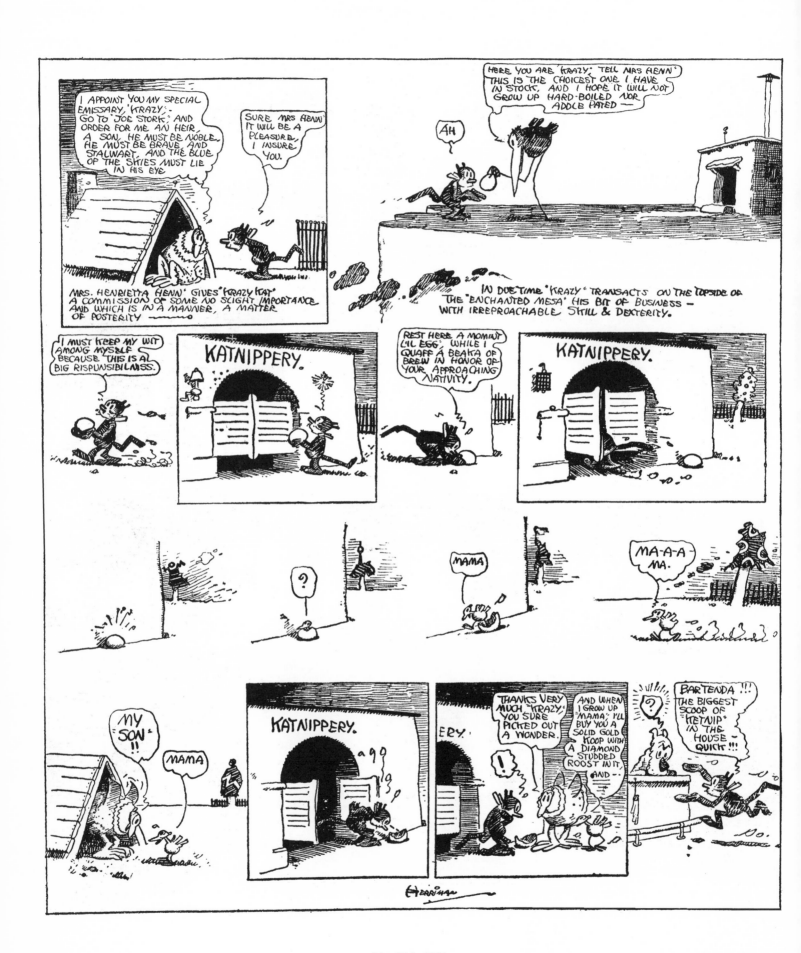

May 15th, 1921.

May 22nd, 1921.

May 29th, 1921.

June 5th, 1921.

June 12th, 1921.

June 19th, 1921.

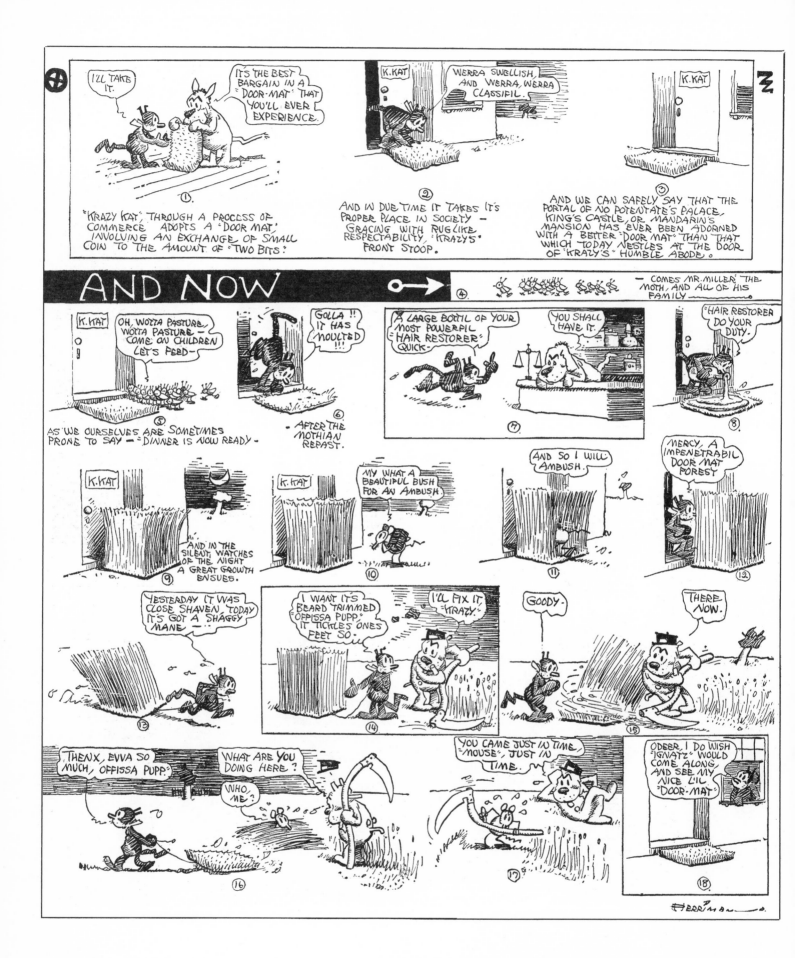

June 26th, 1921.

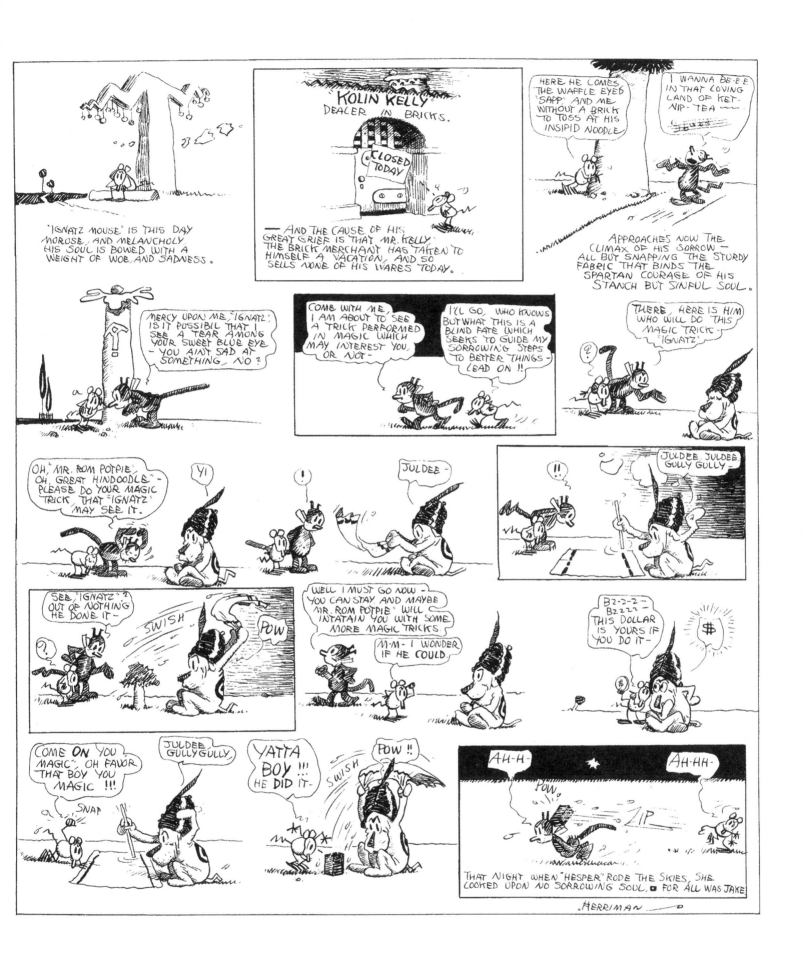

July 3rd, 1921.

July 10th, 1921.

July 17th, 1921.

NIGHT OVERTAKES "KRAZY" FAR AFIELD AND HIS NIMBLE MIND TURNS TO THOUGHTS OF SLUMBER ——

WHEREUPON HE SPREADS HIS SHROUD, GETS UNDER, AND COMMENDS HIS SPIRIT TO "MORPHEUS" ——

"PASQUALE PORKUPINE", FULL OF SLUMBER, BUT WITHOUT A SHROUD IS ALSO OVERTAKEN BY NIGHT.

HIS FRIENDLY NATURE SUGGESTS THAT HE SHARE "KRAZY'S" KOZY KIVEST — WHICH HE DOES —

WHO ARE WE TO SAY THAT SLEEPING WITH A PORCUPINE DID IT —— • ALL WE CAN SAY IS THAT IT'S DERN FUNNY THAT POOR OLD "KAT" SHOULD HAVE THIS KIND OF A DREAM —— USE YOUR OWN JUDGMENT ——

IT STARTED OFF WITH A SPANISH BAYONET BUSH SPROUTING UNDER HIS BED —— ETC.

SOFT PINK CLOUD

HO·HM·M — TIME FOR ME TO BE UP AND MOVING —

HAVE YOU SEEN "KRAZY" MR. PORKUPINE?

YES, HE'S RIGHT OVER THERE ASLEEP.

July 24th, 1921.

148.

July 31st, 1921.

August 7th, 1921.

August 14th, 1921.

August 21st, 1921.

August 28th, 1921.

153.

September 4th, 1921.

September 11th, 1921.

September 18th, 1921.

September 25th, 1921.

157.

October 2nd, 1921.

October 9th, 1921.

October 16th, 1921.

October 23rd, 1921.

"KRAZY" FARES FORTH, BEARING A BASKET OF BEANS — WHITHER, WE KNOW NOT — IT'S NONE OF OUR DERN BUSINESS.

HE JOURNEY'S LONG, AND SO ACQUIRES A BIT OF FATIGUE.

UPON WHICH HE IS MOVED TO SLUMBER, IN THE UMBRAGE OF THE OLD SMOKE TREE

BEHOLD! "IGNATZ" LIKEWISE FARES FORTH, BEARING A BASKET, CONTAINING NOTHING. HENCE EMPTY.

TRAVELLING LIGHTLY HE SUFFERS NO FATIGUE

AND IN TIME ARRIVES, ACUTELY AWAKE, TO THE OLD SMOKE TREE, AND FINDS "KRAZY" DEEPLY ASNOOZE

HIS EVIL SOUL PROMPTS HIM TO SIN.

SO WITH UTTER ABANDON, HE SHATTERS THE SEVENTH COMMANDMENT — A GREAT BEAN ROBBERY TRANSPIRES.

THEN — HE PASSES ON — BEARING A BASKET OF ILL-GOTTEN BEANS.

AH, BUT· "WEIGHT" THAT SINISTER FORCE WHICH RECOGNIZES NEITHER GOOD, NOR EVIL AT LAST FILLS HIS LAWLESS LEGS, AND LIMBS WITH LASSITUDE.

WHICH BIDS HIM HALT!!!

WHERE UPON HE TOO LAPSES INTO A STATE OF SNOREFUL SLUMBER.

BUT, HARK FROM THE BASKET, A BEAN'S VOICE BOOMS — "WILLI MENDOZA" THE MEXICAN BEAN PATRIOT EXUDES AN ORATION.

THE GREAT "BEAN EXODUS"·

BACK TO KRAZY'S BASKET· THEIR CHOSEN ABODE.

REVIVED, REFRESHED, STRONG AGAIN OF LIMB, "KRAZY" FARES FORTH, BEARING A BASKET OF BEANS — WHITHER, WE KNOW NOT — NONE OF OUR DERN BUSINESS ——

October 30th, 1921.

November 6th, 1921.

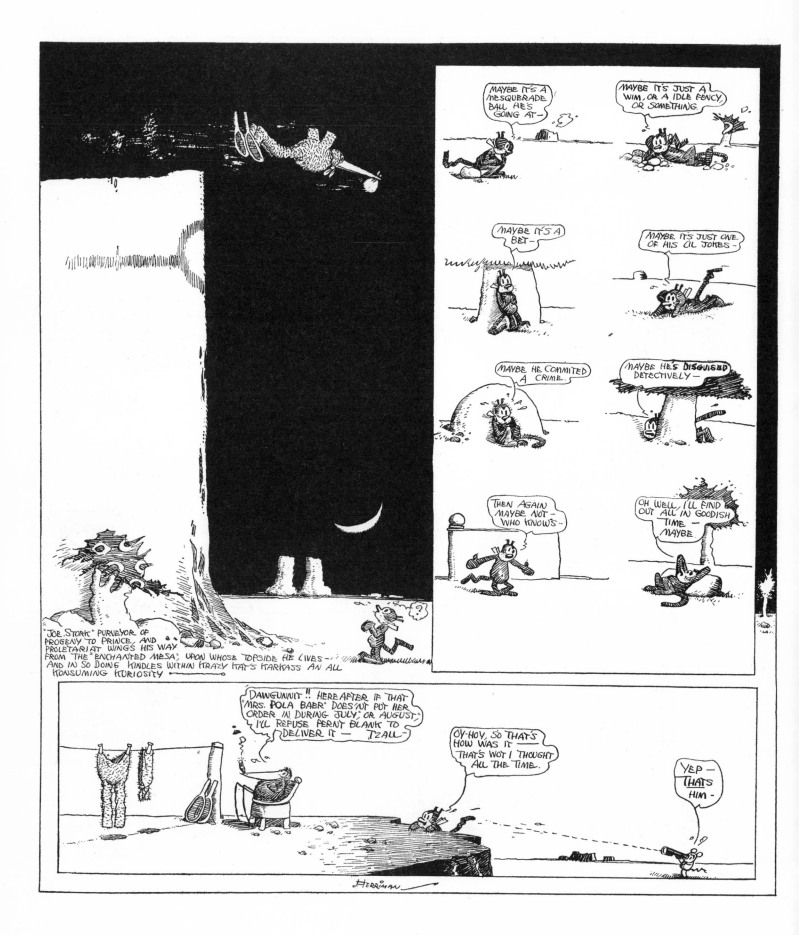

November 13th, 1921.

November 20th, 1921.

November 27th, 1921.

December 4th, 1921.

December 11th, 1921.

December 18th, 1921.

December 25th, 1921.

Nothing is known about this splendiferous undated Herriman piece (from the collection of C. Ware by way of C. Faucher) except what can be conjectured from its contents — so let us conjecture away. Herriman appears to have drawn it for one Antoine Roberge (hence "Tony"), seen twice here, once in poster form and once in "real-life" form, evidently an opera singer. The Metropolitan Opera House is presumably the New York City landmark which stood at West 39th Street and Broadway until the mid-1960s, when it relocated to Lincoln Center Plaza. This scene, however, must take place in Los Angeles since Offissa Pupp's puzzlement likely hinges on a misreading of "Figaro" as "Figueroa," a Los Angeles street that is indeed five miles (if not quite on the other end of town) from the well-traveled S. Highland Avenue. Roberge's brooding apprehension in re "that vulgar 'Peterson'" may refer to a mutual acquaintance (note the Herrimanesque pun, using "operate" to mean "sing" or "perform") — or possibly, given his apparent vaudevillian inclination contumeliously to pelt Roberge with rotten fruit ("second-hand persimmons" and "no count 'tomatusses'"), a critic. Note also a rare instance of racial-stereotype humor on Herriman's part in the diminutive character holding Madame Rita Roberge's train. "Bordeaux" presumably refers to Roberge's city of origin; a "bulbul," even though it looks like another bit of whimsical Herrimanesque wordplay, is in fact an African/Asian songbird that is popular as a cage bird in the Middle East — and thus a useful term of admiration for a singer. —K.T.

The IGNATZ MOUSE DEBAFFLER PAGE.

Eagle-eyed readers of this volume will notice that there are no strips for 2/15/1920, 4/11/1920, and 1/16/1921. This is because in the runs of newspaper tearsheets we've been able to find, those dates carried reprints of earlier strips (respectively 11/16/1919, 12/21/19, and 1/11/1920). Because of the fact that different papers sometimes ran strips on different weeks (Mike Wilbur of Diamond International Galleries, who fortuitously happened to be processing some tearsheets for this period, found one strip from this period with three different dates), dating *Kat* Sundays is not an exact science and some collector may yet turn up with original strips for these three dates, but in the meantime, we're going to assume that Herriman did no new strips for those three dates, and papers were left to fill the space as they saw fit.

On to this volume's debaffling, which combines Bill Blackbeard's original notes with new debafflement courtesy of Jeet Heer and Michael Tisserand.

1/5/19: In the 19th and early 20th century, saloons, such as the one Krazy patronizes in the last panel, often offered a free lunch for anyone who purchased at least one drink.

1/12/19: "Blind pig" was American slang for a speakeasy during the Prohibition era; the actual pig bumbershot by Krazy on this page will become a recurrent Coconino character, one Pedro Puerco, during the course of the year. And surely there is some irony in the fact that a pig, an animal faithful Muslims are not allowed to eat, asks for "alms in the name of Allah."

1/26/19: Here appears just one of the Uncle Tom Kats that inhabited Coconino over the years, including an older Uncle Tom Kat with a fluffy white beard who resided in a cotton field. In Krazy Kat, his sports cartoons and his specialty art, Herriman frequently evoked Harriet Beecher Stowe's anti-slavery novel.

2/23/19: "Ko woodis" is Krazy-talk for "Quo vadis?," Latin for "Whither goest thou?" (or, more contemporaneously, "Where are you going?") and the title of Henryk Sienkiewicz's famous historical novel, whose first film adaptation was released in 1912.

3/2/19: "Oh-hoh — A 'Hickey'— Looks like a good one too —" The best cigar in the store is a product of the Hickey Brothers Inc. cigar dynasty. Based in Davenport, Iowa, the Hickey company claimed its stores and hotel stands "ringed the nation like a giant cigar band."

3/23/19: This page, which explains why bananas cluster together, is one of several strips where Herriman did a riff on the "Just So" stories of Rudyard Kipling, a writer to whom the cartoonist occasionally alluded in other ways as well. See also 11/19/19.

4/6/19: In this outstanding episode we find that Krazy is an antic tease, suffused with guile, at one with the naïve innocent we commonly discern in this creature.

4/20/19: "The sage of Karnak": Karnak is a real place, the largest temple complex built by the ancient Egyptians. Comics fans may know "Karnak" as a Fantastic Four villain; the Johnny Carson swami spelled his name "Carnac," by the way.

6/1/19: "In the swit pie & pie" is from the 1868 hymn "In the Sweet By and By," written by S. Fillmore Bellett, with music by Joseph P. Webster.

7/6/19: Jack "Kid" Wolf, a Jewish boxer from Cleveland, Ohio, battled his way to the first Junior Featherweight Champion of the World title.

7/20/19: "I fear his love for me is dying — he spermed me." Is it too much to see a pun in this love-themed episode?

8/3/19: "I wunna 'who's' kissing him now?" With "him" replacing "her," a reference to one of the more popular songs of the year.

8/24/19: In the explosive era before flash bulbs, news photographers had to rely for illumination on a self-igniting tray of brightly colored flash powder which had to be set off with every snapshot snapped.

10/5/19: A film made from John Fox's 1909 best-selling novel, *The Trail of the Lonesome Pine*, was a minor hit in 1919 and may have suggested the theme of this episode to our artist.

11/2/19: "After the Ball" is indeed an old song for Krazy. Charles K. Harris, famed as "the king of the tear jerkers," wrote the Tin Pan Alley waltz in 1891.

11/9/19: "McNamaran elates" is surely an allusion to Herriman's fellow cartoonist Tom McNamara.

11/23/19: "My goodness, it's at the old hunted house, where nobody lives." This Prohibition tale also reveals Herriman's deep knowledge of Navajo beliefs. The tree bark-and-mud hogan is a sacred dwelling; if someone dies in a hogan, the structure is abandoned and eventually destroyed.

12/28/19: "Celuloid [sic] dicky": a false formal shirt front, much less expensive than an actual "stiff shirt," as worn with a rented formal suit, commonly associated with social climbers, actors, con men, cartoonists and comic book editors and publishers, and their brother accountants.

Herriman made no direct references in his comics to his upbringing in New Orleans. However, a single image of Krazy Kat mocking royalty — with help of an umbrella and tomato-can crown — suggests the Carnival processions he surely witnessed during the first decade of his boyhood.

3/7/20: It is worth calling the reader's attention to Herriman's delicious realization that angelic mice would have bat wings in their afterlife, a point that could be missed in the small size publishing exigencies dictate for these pages. This strip also reflects the post-war surge of interest in spiritualism, and a recent *Saturday Evening Post* story by a medium named Pearl Curran, whose prose was reportedly dictated to her from beyond, via Ouija Board.

3/14/20: The Japanese notion of mokusatsu, or silent contempt, is also translated to "killing with silence." Herriman likely knew the word because of his friend Harry Carr, a Los Angeles Times writer who worked extensively in Asia.

3/21/20: "Y' bald faced gazooni." "Gazooni" is a very rare insult, perhaps coined by Herriman. The only other known reference is in P.G. Wodehouse's 1923 novel *Leave it to Psmith*, where a character exclaims, "You dish faced gazooni"! We know that Wodehouse was a Herriman reader.

3/28/20: It is assumed the reader will keep the bogy of Prohibition in mind in reading these "Kats" from the 1920s: Even to Herriman, forbidden alcohol came to seem mystical, mysterious, and enchanting — as it was clearly a practical commodity to Mr. I. Mouse. Note also 4/11: Sometimes liquor appears to be prohibited in Coconino County, sometimes not. (In 4/25, the camel represents the Prohibition Party, actually a viable political organization in the period.)

8/8/20: A few *Kat* pages were published only in 9 ½" x 8 ½" size in 1920, not much larger than their format here, and "Ent Tewbby's" headgear in the first panel appears to have been heavily "retouched" in a proof of that size by Hearst staffers for some unknown reason. The blotchy effect is not of our ham handed doing, rest assured.

8/22/20: This story of Krazy Kat's jazz party, which attracted Coconino County's elite and bontons alike, was published on August 22, 1920 — George Herriman's 40th birthday. There are no records of how Herriman himself celebrated the day, although two years later another birthday party for Herriman was held in real-life Arizona, featuring such luminaries as cartoonists Jimmy Swinnerton and Rudy Dirks, as well as the photographer Dorothea Lange and her husband, the painter Maynard Dixon.

9/12/20: Just six days before this strip appeared, heavyweight boxing champion of the world Jack Dempsey defended his title against challenger Billy Miske. Dempsey made short work of it, knocking out Miske in the third round.

9/19/20: To reiterate for latecomers, in 1920s urban slang, a "dornick" was a brick.

9/26/20: Stiff opera hats could be folded up and carried flat in the 1920s. While many large department stores sent change from a central cashier to various counters via an overhead system of wires and baskets on wheels, these rarely zipped as close to customers' heads as they do here.

10/17/20: Ignatz's use of an ethnic slur against Mock Duck betrays a prevailing prejudice against Asian-Amerians, who were characterized in Hearst papers (and elsewhere) as part of a menacing "yellow horde" of immigrant invaders. It's a rare cringe-worthy moment in *Krazy Kat*, but it should be noted that Herriman places the offensive term only in the language of the ruffian Ignatz.

11/7/20: Yes, Herriman used it, and the name he gives the widow Pelona is not accidental. ("Marijuana" signs and references are to be found in Kat art through the next twenty-five years.)

11/14/20: The "League of Relations" and the "League of Bricks" echo the League of Nations, which held its first council meeting in Paris earlier that year, and met for its first General Assembly in Geneva on November 15, 1920, the day after this comic appeared.

1/9/21: "Full set of Dinny Galls" Donegals, a style of sideburns, with ultimate reference to northeastern Ireland. Wendel Kiefer, referenced more than once in *Krazy Kat* strips, must have been a personal acquaintance of Herriman's as all efforts to identify him have been in vain.

2/13/21: This rumbustious page depicts a Ku-Kluk-kloaked vigilante attack on censors and prohibitionists (i.e., types that used to be called "bluenoses," hence the thematic wordplay at frolic here). Turns the anti-fun leaguers' preferred tactics around: riding them out of town on a rail for a change. An unusually direct political and social statement by Herriman. (See 3/13/21 as well).

2/20/21: "Kickapoo": An Indian tribal name (like Pottawottamine: see 6/12/21) that has long aroused the risibilities of cartoonists, notably Al Capp and Roy Crane. As for the promised rematch (last panel), it seems never to have taken place.

2/27/21: A wondrous example of one of Herriman's grand themes: the unreliability of color as a way to discern identity. Here, Krazy Kat frets about social position and laments being associated with "li'l Eetiyopian mice." Herriman also frequently employs coffee to describe racial coloring, such as Krazy's reference here to a "koffa-kullid kickipoo." Compare Krazy's disdain for a black Ignatz to Ignatz's infatuation with a white-washed Krazy on 10/16/21.

3/6/21: "Gauntlets" (gloves) and "ulster" (a coat) are the terms referred to here by Krazy: once these were essential motoring accoutrements for the well-to-do. (Note the passing reappearance of Anatole Wuff at the close.)

3/20/21: An innovation of the time, smaller and less-expensive grand style pianos were called "baby grands," hence the gag follow-through here. (Note a rare Herriman misspelling—"believe"—in the 4th panel.)

4/3/21: Omy Khiyi is a reference to Omar Khayyám (1048-1131), a Persian philosopher and poet. Khayyam's work enjoyed an English language vogue in the late 19th and early 20th century thanks to Edward Fitzgerald's translation, *The Rubáiyát of Omar Khayyám* (1859).

4/17/21: "Bastante," meaning "enough" in Spanish, has become a common way for Herriman to end his page.

5/8/21: Electricity was still a novelty in many American homes (particularly rural ones, like Krazy's) in 1921. "Where ever you go, 'Moose,' there will I also go" is a variation on a famous line from the Book of Ruth: "Wherever you go, I will go" (Ruth 1:16).

6/12/21: Having a "good cellar" in Prohibition America meant having a great private stash of booze below decks.

7/3/21: "Hesper": Hesperides.

9/11/21: Note to West Coast readers: if ye would wot of lightning bugs, ask of their nature in converse with friends who hie from east of the deadly deserts....

9/18/21: "Roox": Rooks. "Irish" crows. "Chimney Butte" is almost certainly a reference to George W. Ogden's *The Duke of Chimney Butte*, the movie version of which (directed by Frank Borzage) was released that same year.

11/13/21: Wilson "Pinky" Springer was an old colleague and friend of Herriman's from his *Los Angeles Examiner* days; your Debaffler has so far been unable to locate the other two names, who undoubtedly were also Herriman cronies.

11/20/21: "John Einberg," et al. Doubtless cronies of Mr. Herriman here enshrined in newsprint.

12/11/21: Herriman inserts a plug for the latest Hal Roach movie, "I Do," featuring Harold Lloyd.

A Kat Library, in progress.

All volumes edited by Bill Blackbeard (with some assistance by Derya Ataker, Jeet Heer, and Kim Thompson) and designed by Chris Ware, except *The Kat Who Walked in Beauty*, edited by Derya Ataker and designed by Jacob Covey.

Krazy + Ignatz 1916-1918.

"Love in a Kestle or Love in a Hut." The newest release goes back to the past with the first three years of Sundays! $24.99.

Krazy + Ignatz 1925-1926.

"There Is a Happy Lend Fur-Fur Away." The original first release in the series, with a gallery of supplements. $19.95.

Krazy + Ignatz 1927-1928

"Love Letters in Ancient Brick." Two more years of Sundays plus Herriman's "Embarrassing Moments" panels. $19.95.

Krazy + Ignatz 1929-1930.

"A Mice, a Brick, a Lovely Night." A more flexible layout replaces the earelier "grid" format for even better-looking pages. $19.95.

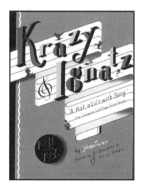

Krazy + Ignatz 1931-1932.

"A Kat A'Lilt With Song." Special bonus: Includes a 20-page portfolio of the 1931 daily strip. $19.95.

Krazy + Ignatz 1933-1934.

"Necromancy by the Blue Bean Bush." Includes the most obscure and hardest to find full-page strips for the first time. $19.95.

Krazy + Ignatz 1935-1936.

"A Wild Warmth of Chromatic Gravy." The first in color, plus Jeet Heer's article on Herriman's ethnicity. $19.95.

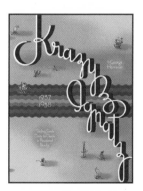

Krazy + Ignatz 1937-1938.

"Shifting Sands Dust Its Cheeks in Powdered Beauty." More full-color strips, plus rarely seen Herriman paintings. $19.95.

Krazy + Ignatz 1939-1940.

"A Brick Stuffed with Moom-bims." Jeet Heer's analysis of Herriman's use of color printing in his work. $19.95.

Krazy + Ignatz 1941-1942.

"A Ragout of Raspberries." Two more years of color strips, Jeet Heer on Herriman's language, and more. $19.95.

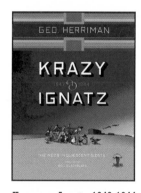

Krazy + Ignatz 1943-1944.

"He Nods in Quiescent Siesta." Page after page of hand-colored originals, an essay on Herriman's last days, more. $19.99.

Krazy + Ignatz 1925-1934 + 1935-1944 hardcover.

These collector's edition library hardcover "bricks" contain the first ten books between them, but without the paperback covers. $75.00 and $95.00 respectively.

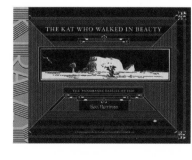

The Kat Who Walked In Beauty.

A unique, 15" x 11", standalone hardcover volume that collects many rare "oversized" dailies (amost as dense as Sundays) from the 1910s and 1920s — plus Herriman's illustrations for the famous *Krazy Kat Jazz* pantomime ballet. $29.95.